ENCOUNTER IN THE SPIRIT

ANDREW WINGATE

ENCOUNTER IN THE SPIRIT

Muslim-Christian Dialogue in Practice

BOOK SERIES

WCC Publications, Geneva

Second edition June 1991

Cover design: Rob Lucas

ISBN 2-8254-0944-8

© 1988 WCC Publications, World Council of Churches, 150 route de Ferney,
1211 Geneva 20, Switzerland

No. 39 in the Risk book series

Printed in Switzerland

Table of contents

Preface

I am a Muslim, and a dedicated servant of Allah. I follow the five pillars of Islam, those of testimony to the Oneness of God, regular prayer, acts of charity, pilgrimage to Mecca, and fasting during Ramadan. I and other Muslims follow the Qur'an and Hadith. In the Qur'an comes the revelation; "Say ye: 'We believe in Allah, and the revelation given to us, and to Abraham, Ismail, Isaac, Jacob and the Tribes, and that given to Moses and Jesus and that given to all the Prophets from their Lord. We make no difference between one and another of them, and we bow to Allah (in Islam)'" (Sura 2.136).

I first met Andrew Wingate in the meeting room attached to one of the Birmingham mosques. We met again at a meeting in Handsworth, where we had discussions about the riots in that area, and considered ways to heal the wounds of the district, and the destruction caused amongst the communities of the area. I believe deeply in the need for the involvement of all communities, regardless of creed, sex and nationality, in building up good will and the desire to live together, whilst letting each one be true to one's own faith. Love and mutual service should be at the heart of this sense of togetherness.

We have had a series of meetings, in Queen's College, in my house, and elsewhere. People have come from many parts of the world including Sri Lanka, India, Sweden, East and West Germany. We all agree that in this world, we are "on probation". We need to channel our energies towards mutual tolerance and understanding. We should respect the integrity and feeling of followers of other faiths. We must preach such tolerance when we are with people of our own faith, to help heal the historical divisions between us. This is what I have been trying to do. There are differences between religions, but these can be left for the judgment of Almighty God, on the judgment day. What we are required to do is to contribute together towards the unity of humanity, and to build up harmony and tranquillity in this world.

This will mean involvement together in the eradication of poverty and, through prayer and practical action, in joint efforts against the consequences of natural and human-made disasters. We should remember always the words of the Qur'an: "On no soul doth Allah place a burden greater than it can bear" (Sura 2.86).

I was brought up from the time of my schooldays, in Gujarat (in Bombay Presidency, as it then was), in India, to campaign for justice for the powerless, in terms of education, the basic necessities of life, and health and all human rights. The rich and selfish often work against such justice. So does the lack of understanding between different religions, which makes millions blind. Love needs to replace hatred in human hearts. Central to this is prayer which is at the heart of all religions. It enables us to relate to God, ourselves and others, so that we can see the way to peace and harmony. It shows us "the straight way". This has been the secret of whatever we have been able to do.

With the help of Allah, I was enabled to take part in the Irina vigil, helping my friend Dick Rogers. I asked Andrew and Queen's to give their support, and by perseverance and prayers, the doors were opened for Irina, and now countless others. In this movement we are glad we could play a small part. I much treasure a letter written to me by Dick Rogers at the time, thanking me and my wife and our "lovely family" for our kindness to him and to the cause of Irina's release. It was a wonderful thing to meet her in person when she visited Birmingham earlier this year.

So I and my family have continued our friendship and association with Queen's friends. Allah has blessed us, and we have achieved something, however small, through his grace. We believe together in the right of every individual to practise alone, or with others, what his or her faith demands of one, and in accordance with one's conscience. Social integration, and not disintegration, should be the goal of our life. Sharing together with people of different faiths is the right way forward. Only in this way can we be, as the Qur'an says, worthy of being called "vicegerents" on earth for God.

The onus rests on all people of faith. Readers of the Torah, the New Testament, the Qur'an, the Upanishads, the Vedas, and the teachings of the Buddha, and others, will be required to give account on the judgment day, on how they have lived in this world and followed their scriptures.

I value much my links with students from Queen's College whom Andrew has introduced to me. Recently I invited some of them to come and join my family in breaking the fast of

Ramadan, a high point in the Muslim year. Several of them had fasted too. For us there was real joy in this sharing, and Martin, one of these students whom I have got to know particularly well, wrote to me: "We are all so grateful for your friendship", and this meant a lot to me.

I would therefore like to commend to your reading this book written by Andrew, which is a record of our experiences together, and what we have learnt, and continue to learn from each other. We hope that, by publishing these things, other Muslims and Christians, and indeed people of all faiths, may be encouraged to follow a similar path in their own places, to build up the mutual understanding and good will that we all long for.

A. MAJID KHAN QAZI
BIRMINGHAM, UK

Preface to the Second Edition

The first edition of this book came out at the end of 1988. Without our knowing it at the time, this was shortly before a kairos period in Muslim-Christian relations. As I have written earlier, one of the important aspects of interfaith meeting is not knowing what is going to be round the corner. Its original release coincided with the publication of a much more famous — and infamous! — book, *The Satanic Verses* by Salmaan Rushdie. While this affair was still unresolved, in August 1990, Kuwait was invaded and annexed by Saddam Hussein. The ensuing Gulf war, involving Western and Arab nations, produced the great danger of raising further walls of suspicion, fear and hatred, between Christians and Muslims. The second edition comes out in the aftermath of this war, where there has been an uneasy cease-fire, and civil war within Iraq. Kuwait has been "liberated" but the search for peace has only just begun. The need for real encounter between Muslims and Christians, as illustrated in this book, becomes all the more important in a world where Christian-Muslim relationships have become one of the most critical issues of our time. Are they to be relationships of meeting, understanding, respect, and imaginative new beginnings, or are they to be those of confrontation, mutual vilification, and hatred? After the collapse of communism, is the new bogey to be Islam, as many expect? The new edition of this book is offered as a small contribution to preventing this happening.

1. Background
of the Encounter

Iqbal[1] is an orthodox Muslim who lives with his extended
family, much as he might in Pakistan, in a run-down inner-city
terraced house in Birmingham. He has periodic employment as
a machine fitter, and gives all his spare time to teaching the
Qur'an to Muslim children. He is also busy learning the Qur'an
by heart. He is one of a small group of such Muslims, all of
them poor economically and socially, but rich in their ability to
articulate their faith, who live their obvious spirituality, with
whom I have made friends over the last few years, and with
whom I have associated a group of students from Queen's
Theological College, where I was on the staff. After a meeting
and a meal shared in his house, Iqbal, a man in his thirties,
about the age of most of our students, but in other ways from
such a different world, took a deep breath and, making clear that
he was saying something important to him and not particularly
easy for him to say because of his orthodoxy, said: "This
journey we have embarked upon together is a very important
one which God is calling us to — and we must not let it go."

He acknowledged here something I too have felt — that what
we have been engaged in is not just a formal "dialogue", but a
real "encounter in the Spirit", and something which has been
truly "converting" for a number of us involved in it, though we
remain Muslims and Christians as we began. One of the Muslim
brothers (and this is the word I naturally use of them now),
commenting on a particular discussion about ethics, said that he
partly agreed with what a Muslim brother had said on the
question at issue, partly with "Brother John" (a Christian
student), an ex-headmaster in his late forties. I felt here we had
passed a significant point, where division was breaking down,
and we were listening to each other, struggling with common
issues of faith and practice.

Another significant moment came when one day Iqbal said,
again weighing his words, that I myself and a number of our
students were, as the Christians we are, more "Muslim" than
most Muslims he knew! Another Muslim friend described one
of our students — and all the more significantly a woman in her
thirties — as "having an old spirit". Puzzled, I asked him what
this meant. With a twinkle in his eye, because we had had a long

---

[1] The names here are pseudonyms.

discussion about the Holy Spirit, he said: "Wise, you know — with the Holy Spirit!" These moments, I think, show the depth of trust that has built up. We are relating "as people to people", not as "representatives of one faith to representatives of another". We are, I believe, relating under the one God, with the Spirit as the unseen third party, the go-between.

I would like to describe this journey in some detail, as an encouragement to others to enter on such a road. It is, in a way, quite ordinary but, in the eyes of those who have taken part, it is recognized in its own way as extraordinary. It may happen often, and surely could. I find it happens perhaps rather less than general discussions "about" dialogue, judging by the interest it raises when I talk about it. And so, reluctantly in some ways, because it is not easy to give to a wider audience something very personal and "sacred" to those involved, I will tell this story, and then make some general observations from my experience of such encounters, as pointers to others who feel led in such directions.

Before beginning the story, I will make three preliminary points as background. The first is about myself, since what we bring to any such meeting is ourselves and the experiences we have had, and these are what God has given us to use. The second is a brief outline of the context of Birmingham since it is important to remember that all meetings take place in a context which should be understood, if it is not to be merely academic discussion. The third is about the particular climate for such interfaith meeting in a place like Birmingham.

First, about myself. In my theological training for the Anglican ministry from 1970 to 1972, I think I completed the course without at any point being made aware of the existence of any other faiths except Judaism. And this was not because of any wish to encourage us to study contemporary Judaism, but because of the unavoidable facts that the Old Testament is Jewish scripture, and both Jesus and Paul were Jews. So rapidly have things changed that I do not think this could happen anywhere in England today. I then worked in a parish near Birmingham, where I became aware of racial and cultural questions, but very little of religious ones related to the "immigrant" population, as was the word then (the word is rarely used today, and rightly so, as increasingly Asian people of other faiths have been born in Britain — again, how quickly things change!). From there, I went to join the staff of the Tamil Nadu Theological Seminary, in Madurai, South India. There "dialogue" was very much on the agenda of theological training, and I also had my personal exposure to other faiths, both Hinduism and Islam, during my seven years there. This was added to my own family situation; my sister married a Pakistani Muslim in England, and I now have a Muslim sister and two Muslim nephews.

My time in India convinced me that we come to understand other faiths not from books and texts, but from meeting people; that lack of academic background in this particular area is not necessarily a disadvantage, since one knows one does not know the answers, and can listen the more. And we meet with *people* who follow Hinduism or Islam, not with Hinduism and Islam. I became fascinated with the complexity of Hinduism, as I met it through its people. Within ten miles of Madurai, we can meet those who follow the highest form of philosophical Hinduism, those who are far on the path of meditative spirituality on the one hand — and how often in the West, we see only this as Hinduism! — and on the other, those who practise animal sacrifice, who fall down on the floor and worship the God who has possessed spirit-filled women with staring eyes, and those who offer their children to a priest who fills their ears with ash (*vibuthi*) as part of a ritual in an open-air altar under a sacred tree. And both are Hinduism. So we must take people seriously, and what each says about his or her faith and practice, and not come with preconceived ideas about what they should be saying and what we should be seeing. I certainly grew to respect those of other faiths more. And where I saw things that were good and true, things that, if they had been in the character of, or done by, Christians, I would have said were the fruits of the Spirit, I could not de-link them from the faith that these people expressed and practised. At the same time, I understood more clearly than I had ever done before what is most central to my Christian faith, and what is distinctive about Christ, as I was led to articulate it more in contact with others. In all, the time in India was, for me, *the* converting experience of my life in many ways — and it came through being deeply immersed in another culture. My aim in Birmingham has been to try, in a more limited way, to give theological students a chance for some sort of converting experience, such that it may have far-reaching implications for their future ministry.

Next, the context of Birmingham. Birmingham is no longer the city of 1000 trades, the symbol of Victorian industrial prosperity. Birmingham's industrial base declined in the seventies more rapidly than in any other city in the country and unemployment has been as high as 17 percent. This figure hides vast differences, between 4 percent in outer suburbs to over 40 percent in certain areas of the inner city. It conceals, too, differences between age groups, with school-leaver unemployment up to 80 percent in some areas. Things have improved somewhat in the last few years and there is more work around and a greater feeling of confidence. But ethnic minorities have suffered especially from the problems of the city, concentrated as they are in inner-city areas, with the under-investment in recent years in so many areas of life. The proportion of households of New Commonwealth descent (today's jargon for non-white) is now 15 percent in the city as a whole, with 33 percent of births in the city's hospitals. Asians, such as those in our study, are concentrated in certain areas in the inner city, where the mosques, temples and gurdwaras are concentrated also (there are now over 50 mosques in the city, including the Central Mosque, said to be the largest in Europe outside Istanbul). Muslims have come from Bangladesh, different parts of Pakistan, primarily Azad Kashmir and the Punjab, and from the Middle Eastern countries. They were mostly villagers, and this is reflected in their way of life here. Theirs is a different world from that of the other group of Asians, rich and professional, with residences in upper-class areas. The city's private schools have an increasing proportion of children from these families. On the whole, they live apart from the problems of their poorer counterparts, as they would in Asia, and it is perhaps through their religious organizations that they mix at all. Increasingly important to Muslims is the preservation and development of their community life, as well as the handing down of the faith intact through the education of the next generation. This is quite clearly central to them, in everything they do. The same is true of Hindus, in a way that is not normally consciously done in India; teaching of both old and young, congregational worship, explanations of rituals in English, and a common meal together.

And finally, the interfaith context. I would emphasize the great gift it can be to Christians in a city like Birmingham to have such a context, if it is seen in a constructive way. The Indian Christian church is a small minority, varying, in the large states of India, from 30 percent in Kerala, to less than 0.2 percent in Uttar Pradesh. Overall, it is only two-and-a-half percent. A large proportion of its members come from what were originally "untouchable castes", so called. Most were poor. This was three or four generations ago or more. But this does mean that a great deal of history has to be overcome in entering into dialogue with people of faiths from which the Christians were originally converted, many of them through such conversion finding liberation and dignity. Many missionaries in the past taught them that all outside the church live in darkness, and so it is difficult to say suddenly that there may be light outside! Moreover, as a minority, there will always be a fear of assimilation, or of syncretism.

In Birmingham, the situation is different. Asian Christians may be seen in the same way by people of other faiths, but the majority white Christians are thought of as those with influence in society, as the host community. This is evident for them in the way bishops are part of the House of Lords, and state occasions are observed in churches; it is seen at a local level, by the historical buildings so prominent around the city. It is seen by the inherited wealth available to the church, and the part its ministers are thought to have in influencing decisions. A lot of this may be exaggerated and a thing of the past, but the belief is still there. It is likely here that the initiative for establishing links between faiths is likely to come from the Christian side, for these reasons, apart from any possible theological imperative. And such initiatives are important not only religiously but also socially, in a society where racism and prejudice lie so close to the surface. It is important to hold out a welcoming hand to those of other faiths who wish for friendship with the Christian community. This can thereby strengthen them viz-a-viz those whose response to the division in society is to withdraw to an island, supported by fundamentalism of one sort or another. And the results of such meetings, if nothing else, deepening and enriching a more open Christian faith, are to be valued for their own sake, whatever may happen to the Muslim or Hindu friend in the meeting.

It must be acknowledged, however, that initiative is easier for some than for others. The story which follows is a story of an initiative largely from Christian students, and from people with some experience of speaking about their faith. It is far more difficult for hard-pressed Christian minorities, "left behind" in areas which have become largely Asian. Many of those with initiative or age on their side have moved out to the prosperous suburbs, and for the elderly and small congregations still there it is hard enough just to maintain a Christian presence and keep their building going. Clergy are hard-pressed here, too, by the realities of church and society in these areas, and they naturally find the interfaith question difficult, when other faiths are seen as a real threat to the very survival of the Christian faith in these areas, because of their great vigour and, sometimes, evangelical zeal. I am not, therefore, sitting in judgment on those who have not been able to embark on the sort of initiatives I am writing about. I am only concerned to present a positive story, as proof that good things are possible.

I made a return visit to Tamil Nadu Theological Seminary in 1987, to visit students who had left the seminary five years before and attempted an evaluation of their ministry. They had been trained in a very contextual way to relate their theology and ministry to the social and religious realities of their situation. Many of them had little contact with the major faith in the area, Hinduism, being brought up in all-Christian villages, or within exclusively Christian families or social environments. Most left the seminary with some structured experience of relating to those of other faiths. Meeting them after five years, I find that few of them have been able to follow this up in terms of dialogue within their ministry. Communalism has increased considerably in India — conversions to Islam, the problems in the Punjab related to Sikh demands, unrest in Assam because of Muslim immigration, Muslim-Hindu clashes in North India, have all contributed to this. And where Christians are strong, as in parts of South India such as Kanyakumari and Tirunelveli they too have been affected by the growing Hindu self-consciousness. Certain forms of evangelical activity have also given Christians a bad name in some areas. The result is that it is difficult for a pastor to relate closely to Hindus without being made to feel that he is letting down the Christian community. Contact at the ordinary, as opposed to academic, level therefore seems to happen largely only socially. An example is a pastor who deliberately does not buy a daily newspaper so that he can share the one in the public reading room, and so get into conversation with local Hindus; he also does not have his daily wash within his parsonage, but goes to the common well in order to meet others. Even this his parishioners do not like. The other main way forward is by engaging in common social action; this can only be effective if it is alongside Hindus, and there are good examples of this. But in general, I came back all the more convinced that in a place like Birmingham we have a special opportunity which it is important to use.

This applies, too, in the Muslim area. What we have been able to achieve here may be much more difficult or even impossible elsewhere, where inter-religious tension is much sharper, as for example in Nigeria or the Middle East.

2. A Diary of the Encounter

Stimulated by a visit to Queen's Theological College by Kenneth Cracknell, secretary of the committee for relations with people of other faiths of the British Council of Churches, who raised a lively theological debate, I called for a group of volunteers who would like to follow it up with practical experience of other faiths, on the basis of which they could return to the discussion. A group came forward, some of whom had done a little academic study of Islam, some not at all. During the first few months we related to Hindus and Hinduism. This was important in itself, but I do not have room to go into it here. What it did teach us was that it was important, if possible, to stay with one group, and follow things through, and not to jump from here to there. Without this, confidence cannot be built up.

What follows is a diary of some of the meetings experienced through these years. Some of the experiences are those of the whole group, some of myself and one or two others. On the basis of this sample of what has happened through the years I will later offer some general reflections.

1 November 1983: We have decided as a group to try to make a worthwhile and sustained contact with some local Muslims. I go down to the Islamic centre, which is in the inner-city parish area where I am on the staff, taking with me one of our women students, who is the leading student in our group. It is in a highly concentrated Asian area, and is the centre for cultural, social and religious activity which are all inter-related for a Muslim. We are greeted warmly by a tall, thin, bearded Pakistani. His name is Zaheer. I ask for the coordinator of programmes, whom I already know, a retired colonel from the Pakistan army. We are told that he has gone back to Pakistan. I am reminded immediately of the difficulty of keeping up sustained contact. However, we explain who we are and what we want, and, in a short time, we have planned a series of meetings on various subjects, and have been told that they will be "taken", by a British convert, much learned in Islam, somebody to whom they clearly defer. I make it clear to Zaheer that we do want the participation of born-Muslims too, and he assures me that he will be there, and others from Pakistan. We then go on to ask about his work, and he tells us that he is enjoying it there, coordinating programmes and doing social work. But he is on a government employment "scheme" and so he has only another three months' work more since, after a year, he will be replaced by another person — just when he has gained experience and is really into the work! However, he is resigned to this, and has much to get on with. He is already teaching in a mosque school in the evening, when he finishes at the centre. He will find other voluntary work to do in the community, and will also be freer to pursue his Islamic studies. He came to Britain as a teenager, and worked in engineering for some time, before becoming redundant in the general recession. He went back to his home country, in order to deepen his faith and understanding, which he did quite systematically. He had then come back here, having married, and is now settled and happy. He is quite delighted when we show interest in his school and family, and invites us to visit both.

17 November 1983: We hold the meeting, planned above, on "prayer". There is considerable interest in the college, and about 15 of us cram into the small room in the centre, along with the European Muslim speaker, Zaheer, and two others from Pakistan. I have emphasized to the European, whom I have met in preparation, that we are interested in "dialogue". But ominously, there is a conspicuous blackboard! It is very hot in the room, with all of us sitting on the floor. After introductions, the speaker takes over, and lectures for over an hour, at the end of which the blackboard is covered in Arabic, which none of us know! It is very informative about Islamic spirituality, but not what could be called "dialogue"!

Tea was then served by the Pakistanis, which was the only contribution they were able to make to the evening, since they deferred entirely to the speaker's learning. I learnt afterwards from Zaheer that the European was a convert from Catholicism; he had become a Muslim partly at least to shock his parents, as an act of revolt more telling than becoming a Protestant! This came out even more when we had general discussion after tea, which turned into our asking questions, which he answered in a way that showed the superiority of Islam at every point, and also showed he was reacting to a particular form of Christianity, which he assumed was the only form and which appeared to us very much one of his imagination. However, he would not be corrected, nor was he really interested in listening, though he remained both polite and humorous. In the end I called the meeting to an end, and the students left, feeling that there had been no real meeting, and with their prejudices about Islam and its dogmatism confirmed. I felt a little discouraged about where we had started!

1 December 1983: As a follow-up to the previous meeting, we visited the neighbourhood mosque in the largely Asian area of Sparkbrook. Attached to it is a school and a book shop. As always, I wonder at how they can be so welcoming, and so patient with our questions. I ask about this, and they say they feel a clear calling to do something for community in the area and further afield, and opening themselves up to those from the majority community is one way of doing this. Up to 400 children study here two hours an evening, five days a week. We are taken on a tour of their classrooms, and one of our students remarks afterwards that it is like crossing a frontier between continents, walking in from a run-down Birmingham street to find oneself on the North West frontier. We spend time with different classes, and are surprised at the number of girls who are pursuing Urdu, Arabic and Islamic studies. I wonder about the virtue of studying Urdu, since few of them speak it outside the class. And indeed this is a question increasingly occurring to some of those responsible for the teaching; Arabic is crucial because of the Qur'an, and that and teaching about Islam in English may well become the pattern in the future. Many of the students are concerned about the educational method, and wonder how these traditional methods of rote learning contrast with what they are experiencing at day school, by Western methods. All are impressed by the commitment of those involved.

We sit then through the prayers, our women students being allowed to remain at the back, as we witness about a hundred or more men performing their evening prayers. I feel, as always, the beauty and the symmetry of their movements, and the universality of them, as I think of South Indian villages where they follow the same pattern of prayer.

Prayer flowed into relaxed discussion, and we were there for two more hours, and shared tea and biscuits. We talked of education. They were not resentful that little was done in most schools for religious education, but they felt things had improved in some ways. One man said that he had been at school some time ago, and when they asked for a place to pray in, they had been directed to the lavatory. Another, at college, had to pray in his car. But things have greatly improved, and also the Muslims have realized that education is primarily the responsibility of the Muslim community and their families. This is where nurture lies. And Christians should accept the same thing, and nurture children in the Bible and Christian thought and practice, when they are in the community, rather than at school. We feel the strength of their argument, when we think how weak Christian nurture is in so many Christian families and churches! We also wonder whether their own children will always be so cooperative, as they get more and more influenced by their environment here.

2 December 1983: I and my student took up the invitation of Zaheer (see 1 November). We met him waiting for us, outside his house mosque, on a dark winter evening that made the dreary urban surroundings particularly bleak. But large numbers of Muslim children were coming and going, and his welcome and obvious delight that we had come made us feel at home. He exhibited his pupils and their skills to us — they were clearly devoted to him — and then rushed us off to another place where he teaches, less than two miles away, but, in complete contrast, in one of the wealthiest areas of the city. Here, five children gather each evening, members of an extended family, and as bright and shining as the silver and brass ornaments which surround them on all sides. The two fathers have made their money "in Saudi" and now own a video business. Their wives share the housework, one looking after the children, while the other goes to teach. Zaheer, though from such a different background, is very much accepted and loved by the children, and he clearly loves them. The parents respect him for his wisdom and skills. The four boys put on their caps and recited in turn, their sister sitting amongst them. Meanwhile, the mothers talked with us freely, in a way that could not easily happen in South Asia. They emphasized the importance of understanding, and gave, as an example, the question of a Muslim having four wives, so often raised by Westerners. This they saw as a protection for the woman, who would otherwise be bereft if a husband dies in war or famine. This was seen by them as a means of giving security to women.

From there we went to Zaheer's house, a small terraced one, sparse and quite cold, where he uncomplainingly struggles to make ends meet (in fact, I have never heard him complaining about his lot in life). We met his wife and their beautiful daughter. His wife said she could not speak English, but my student, being a woman, could go with her into the kitchen, and there she managed well as she talked and cooked at the same time. They gave us humble food, and also payasam, a special sweet in our honour. As we began to eat, in came Zaheer's mother, a wizened but formidable lady who criticized the payasam and put her daughter-in-law back in her shell. Accompanying her were a cousin and his family. He had a vast great-coat on, and looked as if he had just come off the Himalayas.

Zaheer, referring to his old mother, then said: "In Islam, there is the absolute necessity to honour our parents. Not giving them respect is one of the three things that cannot be forgiven."

"What are the other two?" we asked.

"Adultery and alcoholism. But in both one can repent even at the last moment. And then there is denying Allah. But repentance is never too late, provided there is the intention not to commit the same sin again. Even on our death bed, if we turn to him, there may be mercy. But honouring our parents is crucial. I will tell you a story from the Hadith. These are the traditions about the prophet Muhammad, peace be upon him. We hear there about the prophet Isaac, and how he asked Allah to show him a man who walked close to God. He had looked to every corner of the earth, and never found one. 'Go to the countryside, and I will guide you to one,' instructed Allah. And so off he went, and all he was shown was a man tending two swine. 'Why this man, doing this poor and unclean task. If he were a good Muslim, he would have nothing to do with pigs!' said Isaac puzzled. But Allah replied: 'You asked to see a man who walks close with God. This is he. His parents committed some grave sins, and then died, and were reborn as swine, as a punishment. But still their son remains devoted to them, and tends them day by day.'"

It is a beautiful story, and Zaheer, we found later, loves stories. "Narrative theology"? I am puzzled by the reference here to reincarnation. "Not exactly orthodox Islamic belief", I think, but do not say at this stage in our friendship. It is anyway a powerful illustration. Instead, I said: "For us too, honouring our father and mother is one of the basic ten commandments. It cannot be set aside, even if we think we are honouring God more by doing so," and I recount the passage from the Gospels where Jesus censures those who do not look after their parents and make the excuse that they have vowed to give the money to the temple.

"Yes," said Zaheer, "this central duty is common to both our faiths. And anyway, I owe so much to my mother. I came to Britain as a teenager, with my father, and worked in various factories. After some years, in my twenties I decided to go back to Pakistan, to try really to understand Islam. I stayed a year, and sat there in the class with all the small boys."

"Were you not embarrassed?" I asked, imagining how I would feel. "I was at first, but this I knew I had to do. And, anyway, I was so happy to be reunited with my mother. I was sure that it was her prayers that had sustained me during the years when I had been alone with my father in England. I plan to take her on Haj next year. This, as you know, is the pilgrimage to Mecca. It is the least I can do for her before she dies."

As I saw the old lady in the corner of the room, battered by life, I could hardly believe it possible. But this was what he later did.

"And how did you keep up your faith on your return?" I asked.

"I brought my mother over to help me. And I became a murith, that means a disciple, of a Sheikh in Birmingham. He is a holy man, and he represents the Pir, from Kohat, in the North West Frontier of Pakistan. A Pir is someone who is recognized by us Sufi Muslims as having special spiritual gifts, and healing powers."

"What we, as Christians, would call a saint?"

"Yes, sort of. Disciples gather round him for guidance and teaching, and after he dies, they visit his tomb, and receive all sorts of help. But eat up now, and then I would like to say a prayer."

It was strange, but all academic questions about interfaith prayer seemed to fade away at that moment, and our hands naturally opened, as his did, in praise and thanksgiving. After reciting a little of the Qur'an, he prayed in English, giving thanks for us, and this special meeting, as he called it, and how much we had learnt, both about each other and about God.

All was not finished, however. Next we were off to another friend's house, where, after further discussion, the host also prayed — in Arabic, apologizing for this because of the lateness of the hour (now nearly midnight!). Then Zaheer prayed again, sensitively, in the name of the Prophet, peace be upon him, and of all the prophets, peace be upon them. On other occasions, friends have prayed through Muhammad, peace be upon him, and through Jesus, the Spirit of God. This, it would seem, was to include us in the prayer.

In this second house, our host Nazir was another young and cheerful bearded man. His wife was fast asleep with her child when we went in. She was roused to make the usual, highly scented and very sweet cup of tea. "Don't bother her, let her sleep," we said. But Nazir would have none of that. "It is her duty. In the Islamic culture, she should obey, and anyway you are guests, and we must serve you."

"But does she not mind? She looks so sleepy." "No, it is her duty. You probably think she is oppressed. But in our culture, women have a very clear sphere of authority. She is in control of the home, and what she says goes. In your culture, with women's liberation, you compete for power. We divide it into different areas."

If we had known him better, we might have discussed this difficult subject further. But he initiated a theological discussion. "Please tell me something about the idea of the Holy Spirit. We Muslims believe that the 'other advocate', promised after Jesus, is Muhammad. Here, I have a Bible, tell me what you would say about this passage, as Christians. I have heard only Muslims talk about it before."

He got down a Bible from his shelf, where it was placed between large Arabic tomes. I looked up John 15, and gave a short exposition of the texts there. "The Holy Spirit is crucial for us, as it is a way of understanding that God is with us now, and it is in his power and strength that we are guided in our daily lives, in prayer, and in our search for truth."

They asked then about further biblical texts, such as "Go not, except to the lost sheep of the house of Israel". Not an easy one! I tried to explain. "This appears to have been the original extent of Jesus' ministry. But things did change. Look at the parable of the vineyard."

We read from Matthew's Gospel, how God's vineyard was given to others, because the original owners did not care for it. "But this does not mean that God has eternally rejected the Jewish people, and replaced them with the Gentiles. That is the insight of St Paul. Let us look at Romans 9-11."

We then looked at this text, about how Paul agonized about the ultimate fate of his people, and how he remained sure that they would be grafted in. I was impressed by the way they listened.

As if this was not enough for one night, Zaheer raised the question of the cross: "God always protects his prophets. Jesus was his prophet. How then could he allow him to be destroyed?"

"But it is the cross that shows us that God really enters into evil, which we all agree is here, and gathers it upon himself and, through his resurrection, destroys it in Christ. There has to be a human death, as well as a fully human life, in order to show the depth of God's love."

They both seemed to show a genuine interest in Christian theology.

The evening ended with swapping stories. They told us how the Sheikh had helped them with his prayers, in healing situations. An example was how he had given a *tawiz* (an amulet containing a verse of the Qur'an) to Nazir's wife, which had prevented a miscarriage and ensured a safe delivery. We also heard stories of healing by demons, and I was reminded of India, with the mixture of high theology and popular faith. We were together for several hours. It was all unplanned, but became the basis of our relationship which has followed, as we showed our willingness to go here and there as the Spirit moved!

17 December 1983: I again visited the rich Muslim family with my six-year old son, Matthew, when Zaheer was taking an Arabic class for the five children. Matthew, to his amusement, was immediately enrolled, and given a cap to wear. This gave me the chance to talk to the mother of one of the three children. She was clearly North Indian, and told me how she had been a Sikh, and had converted to Islam at marriage. This had led to her immediately being cast out, and she now did not even know the address of her family, though they were in England. But the Muslim family had accepted her as one of them, and she could not be more full of praise for them. Zaheer came in at this point, and talked of how Guru Nanak had concentrated on the *love* of God, which united all. When he died, the Hindus and Muslims both claimed his body, and brought flowers. It was decided that whoever's flowers remained fresh over night could claim the body. In the morning, the body had gone, and both sets of flowers remained fresh; and so one group was given the shroud, the other the bier. This showed how he was a saint beyond religions. It is the sort of unity that comes from sainthood rooted in the love of God. I added an account of my meeting with Mother Teresa in Agra, and the sort of unity she had created amongst those of all faiths who were present.

23 December 1983: I took Matthew with me on a Christmas visit to Zaheer's family. I am struck again by how much his wife still lives as if she were in Azad Kashmir, with her relatives and her neighbours who are largely from Pakistan. The shops around are mostly Asian, and she very rarely goes to town. Her doctor, too, is an Asian, who speaks to her in Punjabi. (Over the next four years, she has three more children, including the coveted boy. They dominate her life more and more, and so the chances of her learning English diminish further. A student whom I introduce to her later, who faithfully visits every week in order to teach her English, rapidly finds the overwhelming presence of very active, and ever-present young children with few toys to play with, an impossible impediment to learning progress, and wisely she settles for befriending rather than teaching!)

We had a meal together of fish curry, chapattis, and halva. Like the whole Christmas season itself, it seemed to have an almost sacramental quality, with a simplicity and depth of meaning often lost in our so-called "Christian", but secular, Christmas. Zaheer asked me this time to bless the food, and to pray, especially for his daughter, who had had her birthday two days before. I had no hesitation — it seemed entirely right; as I did in India when asked by those of other faiths to pray, I used words appropriate to where they were, but words which I too could pray with full integrity, as a prayer to God the Father, in the Spirit, through Christ, but not necessarily with all these expressed in this direct way. To me, it is no different from praying with anyone in need, such as those you would meet in a hospital or before a funeral, in a normal pastoral ministry, with little or no church connection. You pray for their needs, in words they can cope with. This praying together has been central to the friendship which Zaheer and I have, and is not an experiment in prayer; it flows naturally from the respect we have for each other, and for the faith that motivates each of us. It is based on a strong feeling of unity in the love of God, and has been central to the continuation of our group. We both feel a common vocation to proclaim this to those who come from either side to our meetings, yes, such a unity is possible, from our so different backgrounds!

19 January 1984: Most of our meetings have been primarily with college students, but included also were parishioners from the inner-city parish where I assist. I will describe one such meeting with parishioners. Zaheer came with the two friends mentioned above, Nazir and Iqbal. Iqbal is short, sharp and serious. Very orthodox, yet incongruously wearing a tartan cap, which he did not take off all evening. Nazir was dressed in a light green suit (worn by a Sufi for religious and spiritual gatherings, he explained). In the house we met there was a dog, and it had to be removed before we started, since they did not wish to defile their prayer clothes. Parishioners included both white and Afro-Caribbeans.

Iqbal began the meeting by reciting the Qur'an (he is a teacher of Kirath, recitation). It was the first chapter, which he then translated and interpreted carefully. Zaheer then took over the chairmanship confidently and sensitively (though there were two clergymen present; how many Christian lay people will do that, and have the confidence to do so, even with far more formal education than Zaheer!). Nazir then talked about what Muhammad meant to him, and discussion proceeded with direct questions, centring on the relationship between forgiveness and justice. Iqbal contributed a nice story about a Jewish woman who was observed by Muhammad and his disciples moving her child away from the fire as she cooked for him. He crawled back, but she moved him again and again. Muhammad observed: "As the Jewish woman is doing, so will Allah for us, and hundreds of times more", illustrating God's personal care and patience with us.

One of the Christians, a sensitive woman, made a little speech about how she found Islam a rather sad religion, and spoke of the recent visit we had made to the large central mosque, where she found the worship dignified, but with no joy or colour, and above all no music. The very austerity of the surroundings signified for her the remoteness of God in Islam. This openness was useful, as the Muslims were then able to give their explanations about why things were so, and to speak of their Sufi tradition which provides a different light. They quoted the well-known description of Allah being closer to us than our jugular vein.

Questions followed about Ayatollah Khomeini of Iran, and what he does in the name of Islam. The agenda cannot be predicted in a meeting like this! At first Iqbal tried to be defensive, but then gradually shifted to saying that what he does in accordance with true Islam is good, but there is much that he does merely as a misguided ruler. Zaheer brought the meeting to an end in his inimitable way, with a touching speech about unity and peace, and he and I adjourned to his house for lamb curry and chappati, with four new friends of his. It involved another hour's dialogue. Again I am struck by the open-endedness of these evenings!

19 February 1984: At Nazir's house. About a dozen of us had gathered when news arrived that the next-door family had just heard of the death of a relative in Pakistan. Their spiritual leader, their Sheikh, had arrived to conduct prayers, and so our Muslim friends adjourned next door, leaving one of their number to talk with us. This Sheikh is a very strong presence in the area, a large, bearded, guru-looking figure, who speaks little English, and appears to be a man of few words, but clearly is considered to have great spiritual power. He works in a factory for a living, but has a strong pastoral role, doing things like hospital visiting, praying with the sick at home, giving advice and aids to healing, being the focus of the community, leading them in processions through the city on holy days, and for representing Muslim interests.

This time they wanted to hear from Christians, and not the other way round. One of the students tried to express what Jesus gives us, which we feel is necessary, so that we are not alone in our human frailty. Distinctions were clarified between the Muslim seeing the Qur'an as the word of God, and the Christians seeing the New Testament as the witness to the word of

God who is Jesus. This means the differences the Muslims can point out among the different Gospels, and the contrast between these and the original and lost Injil, are not central, but Jesus himself. We agreed to devote our next meeting to the question "Who is Jesus?", at the request of the Muslims.

There were two further interesting developments. The first was to see the monolith of unanimity breaking down amongst the Muslims, which was a sign of deepening relationships, where they do not need to show they agree together on everything.

One of the Christians asked: "Why do you always sit on the floor?" Nazir replied on behalf of the Muslims: "It is the natural thing to do in our country. It is very relaxing. We therefore continue it here. But there is also a deeper reason. It is so that no man can be above another in the sight of God, and this is a sign, just as when the king arrives at the mosque late, he must sit in the back row, next to his humblest citizen."

"And such equality before Allah applies to all people. This includes Christians and Muslims and Jews. And indeed Hindus and Buddhists, because they too have some sort of knowledge of God," added Zaheer.

Iqbal would not accept it. "I must totally disagree. They worship idols, and have no knowledge of God. Moreover, they have the caste system, which is an abomination. How can you talk of equality, with a religion like that?"

This has been a consistent area of disagreement among them. Zaheer has always shown surprising openness and readiness to include Hindus within the scope of God's grace, also a willingness to include them in his prayers.

The other breakthrough came at the end of the evening when Zaheer asked me to pray, not just with him privately, but with the whole group, twelve Christians and seven Muslims, in the small prayer room in Nazir's terraced house. The British Council of Churches' little book *Shall we pray together*? had come out the previous week. I included a prayer for the bereaved Muslim family next door, and for Beirut where, in the name of our two faiths, people fought and killed. In that context how much our meeting meant! I prayed "In thy name, O Lord". Iqbal, too, prayed on behalf of us all, and we ended with a common meal, supplied by the Muslim family next door.

1 March 1984: Meeting in our house. I went round by car to collect the Muslims. On the way, I stopped at the house of the wealthy family mentioned earlier. The five children were lined up in a row. Zaheer said to one of them, a young boy wearing his cap and little studious glasses: "Please tell uncle what you know of the Qur'an. Recite some verses."

He solemnly knelt down, folded his arms, and rocked backwards and forwards, reciting the Arabic at great length. He was about seven. "That is what I know," he said, looking pleased with himself.

"Do you know the meaning?" "No, but I do know how to pray. I normally go to God's house to do it, but I will do it for you now."

He then went through the full prayer actions, and the whole scene reminded me of seeing the same thing in an Indian village; the son of a wealthy Birmingham business man, unified in faith and practice, with the child of a poor Muslim family, in a hot and dusty village, the teacher in each case beaming with pride as his protege shows off his skill.

Then on, here and there in the car; Nazir we found ill, and went on without him, though he asked us to pray for him. Further delay, while Iqbal stopped to call on a friend. With my Indian sense of time, I was unconcerned — but hoped the others waiting would feel that same way!

I need not have worried, as whatever impatience there may have been evaporated as we greeted each other with the "Salaam alaikkum" words and the traditional three-fold embrace, which is by now natural among us. I am struck by how warm this is amongst the men, but how, of course, our women students are excluded from this, and there are only men from the Muslim side. This is something which is just a reality we have to go along with, and marks strongly the cultural boundaries. Our women can only meet Muslim women on a one-to-one basis, when visiting the house. When I reflect about how much I had been able to learn from the Muslim sisters of my brother-in-law when I visited Pakistan, I feel sad that such an experience is not open to more people. It is having a relative which is the key that opens things up. I find also here in England that my brother-in-law, being a Muslim, and my sister having "embraced Islam", give me a head start in being accepted and shown confidence by other Muslims.

Our discussion this evening centred around the place of Jesus in our personal faith. One of the most valuable aspects from the theological education point of view is that our students — as many over thirty as under thirty in age — are made to speak about the faith that is in them through these encounters. They have to speak about what is central, and about what, strangely enough considering they live in a theological community, is often least talked about. The same applies with a parish group, who are often not used to talking to each other at all about their faith.

What is crucial is that a person speaks of the faith within him, and not just what he or she feels should be said from an orthodox position. This applies to both sides of the discussion, and requires a building up of trust. One student spoke of Jesus being the one who breaks barriers, and goes out to people in love, particularly those least acceptable in society. Jesus was essentially anti-religious, in an institutional sense, and was against rigidity in the moral code. By this, he showed us the character of God, and taught us to enjoy life to the full, and to feel released from slavish obedience, to be able to question tradition. The crucifixion was because people could not accept this love, and revealed God as our friend.

This view was a difficult one to take, not only for the Muslims, but also for many of the Christians. One or two of them found themselves closer to what Iqbal said about Jesus. He saw him as an ideal example, showing us the discipline required for life. He did sit with sinners, but this was to reform them. And Jesus taught a code, because we need a code to live by, and this is what distinguishes us from animals. Limited free will is given to us in following the right path, and life is a trial. What we need to do is to try, and then pray there will be mercy when we fail. We have no choice whether to enter this world, or whether to leave it. What we do have choice about is what to do on our pilgrimage in between. Mercy if we do our best, otherwise justice.

We were then asked about heaven and what it might be like. They gave in a straightforward way a traditional picture of judgment, as seen by a Muslim, with rewards for those who are blessed. As we heard this, I was thinking of another Muslim who said to me recently, the reason why Christians find it hard to understand how so many on either side are giving their lives in Iran and Iraq, and in Afghanistan as well, is that they do not really, deep down, believe in the reward of heaven. Muslims never question this, and that is why they have no fear of death in a Jihad (Holy War), since the reward for them is so clear.

I replied by suggesting that the quality of life in a real community of love was the closest we could get to heaven in this life, and that this was a sign of eternal life as it is and would be. Now we can only see through a glass darkly, but we believe that in the very being of God there is a relationship of love, between God the Father, Son and Spirit. The love that we experience, which mirrors this, with each other and in relationship to God, is ultimate and eternal. It is open to all, and that is the message for the thief beside Jesus on the cross — "Today, you will be with me in paradise." We spoke, too, of the parable of the Great Feast, and of the unexpectedness of who is included.

This they understood, and we went on to a discussion of hell. This they believed in a literal sense, as the necessary corollary of the reality of free will and the justice of God. A number of us found it difficult to insist upon it in their terms, with the necessity of eternal punishment. This Iqbal in particular much wanted to press, and we discussed the parable of the sheep and the goats in Matthew 25, with its reference to being cast into utter darkness. We tried to argue that there is a general revelation of a God of love, through the New Testament, and that this is what we stand by, rather than particular passages (the Muslims find this approach to scripture very difficult, as indeed do some fundamentalist Christians). In the course of this, Iqbal conceded that, though the Injil is lost, he did believe that "most of the New Testament is the original Gospel". I found this somewhat surprising, coming from him, and it showed how far we had moved.

7 March 1984: Went to see Nazir in his sickness, and drank the usual scented tea with him. It was Ash Wednesday, and I had an ash cross on my forehead from the service I had just been to. "What on earth is that?" Nazir asked, fascinated, and I was able to describe its meaning at length.

"You listen well," I observed. "Yes, I am a better listener than talker, and that is my problem."

"It is not a problem. Rather it is an ideal foundation for what we are trying to do together. By really listening, we can understand each other."

"Well, it is what we are trained to do as murith. We listen to our Sheikh, and he leads us stage by stage along the spiritual path."

As he described his discipleship as a Sufi, he spoke much as a Hindu would of his guru. There is a humility about him, and he is conscious of himself as a learner with a long way to go — but with a real intention to make the journey. He remarks that Iqbal would not go along with any of this, since he is "very orthodox". As we left, he asked me to give him a commentary on one of the Gospels, which I promised to do, and he lent me a book called *The Descension of Christ*(!), a title which amused me. It refers to the second coming of Christ, as a sign of the judgment day.

11 March 1984: Zaheer and Nazir came to the eucharist at Queen's College, at their own request. It was good to be there with them, and I think they felt the atmosphere, as we do when we sit in on their prayers. They gently accepted that they could not join in the eucharist, something that is harder for a Hindu to understand since at a temple all can receive the prasadam (blessed food). How different it is in almost every way to relate to Hindus from relating to Muslims, and how often we forget this, as the church puts all "other faiths" together. A woman is preaching this morning, which was interesting for them; their reflection afterwards is that they cannot understand why, if a woman can do that, she cannot be a priest. It should be all or nothing; in Islam it is nothing, but we are somewhere illogically in between.

We adjourned to breakfast in a student's flat, and talked about the meaning of the eucharist, the feeding of the five thousand and so on. Nazir added a story from the Hadith, and Zaheer capped this, from the Qur'an, he said, but in fact it seems it was from the Hadith. One of our students who is knowledgeable in Qur'an said he had noticed how Zaheer in general moves from one to the other and back, prefacing all with "as it says in the Holy Qur'an". It is easy to see how an oral tradition becomes authoritative over time.

17 March 1984: We went to the opening of a Muslim community centre, of which Nazir is the treasurer, and Zaheer social organizer. The community in the particular area of Birmingham has raised £70,000 in less than a year, an amazing achievement considering the proportion of people who are employed. I have seen Nazir with his subscription list, and how unemployed families are giving amounts like £4 a week. Lessons for our stewardship! This function reminded me of many I have been to in India. Very formal, but saved by the humour and amateurishness of the formality! I was with 400 men in the main room. Nazir made a speech about how it was necessary for future Imams to study in English, and to come up from families in England, and not to rely on bringing them from Pakistan. There then followed just the type of stilted, rehearsed speeches in English, from young pupils, that I used to hear in India — but with much more justification here, surely, because Nazir is right.

27 April 1984: I went with Matthew to Zaheer's with Easter eggs. The whole family were clearly happy to see us, and we went with them to visit another Muslim friend, who is suffering from leukemia. He is the man who drives the Sheikh around, and has great strength from his faith in his suffering. His wife is a Hindu convert from Gujarat, cut off from her family. She tells of a dream she has had about a long-dead prophet coming to her and asking for bread. This has been interpreted as a desire for her prayers at a prayer meeting. Zaheer spoke about his friend's suffering, saying it could either be a test or the means of gaining forgiveness for an evil done or, if neither of these, would be compensated for in the next life.

As we sat in the sun, in the backyard of the little house, we talked of a number of things. One was alcoholism, which it seems is becoming a problem among certain Muslim youth. They are warned of the dangers, some listen and some do not. Zaheer adds that the Arabs used to drink a great deal, and the prophet began by saying, do not drink before you come to prayer; only later came the absolute prohibition. Zaheer ended by praying for his friend, and I felt honoured and trusted to be there at such a moment; he asked me, too, to visit his friend in hospital. As we left and went into the streets, three children ran past; Zaheer said spontaneously: "Aren't children wonderful?"

There is something so generous about him. I think of the way he stands outside his house, in his back street, greeting all who pass, white, brown or black, and compare this with the complete anonymity of the well-to-do residential area I live in, where it is unusual for anyone to walk on the road at all, and certainly to greet each other.

10 May 1984: A meeting at Iqbal's, accompanied by a delicious meal of saffron rice, chappatis and meat curry. Iqbal was clearly proud to be host and I felt this evening how privileged we are to have met this trio. Nazir was resplendent in his green with white around his head — the clothes, he insists, not of a Sufi but of a prospective Sufi. Iqbal is as intense as ever, but now losing some of his shyness.

Nazir whispered in my ear: "Iqbal is too serious, and is trying to advance on too many fronts at once — to learn the Qur'an by heart, to learn the skill of intoning it, and to become a scholar in theology. Besides this he works as a taxi-driver, and teaches children, as well as having two of his own. He should specialize."

Zaheer arrives a little late, and we feel his considerable sense of authority as he comes in. In discussion he never dominates, always enables, and brings others in. He is so reliable, a real minister or pastor in the best sense of those words — and yet he has had no theological training! As we look across the room this evening, I whisper to Nazir that this gathering is rather remarkable — the trinity, Iqbal's father, his cousin, and nine of us Christians. Nazir agrees, adding that some would see nothing special, but if we look with the eyes of light, it is remarkable.

For the main part of the evening, we followed our planned topic which was a comparison of St Paul and Abu Bakr, the closest follower of Muhammad and the first caliph. We had given them Acts 9 and 10 to read and asked for their comments; they had given us a small book about Abu Bakr.

"Paul never knew Jesus in the flesh," they pointed out. "Abu Bakr was at Muhammad's side. And so how can we know Paul's witness is true?"

"He had a vision of the risen Lord, on the road to Damascus." We read it to them. And here our Muslim friends differed on the validity they would give to visions.

Iqbal said: "The development of tradition through visions is not possible in Islam." He was quite dogmatic about it.

Nazir disagreed emphatically. "Abu Bakr put together fragments of the Qur'an, before it was lost, because he followed a vision."

Zaheer asked: "How can we judge a vision?"

One of us suggested: "A community should be involved in this, as with St Paul and the church. Also there should be a visible change in one's life as a result."

Another Christian, a West German Lutheran who is staying with us, added: "The emphasis should not be on the vision itself and its content, but on the grace of God. This is where Paul puts it in his Epistles."

We compared, too, the common pattern of involvement and withdrawal in the two men, and suggested this is a mark of the journey to sainthood. Another question was whether a saint had to be poor. Abu Bakr made that gesture of renunciation at first. The important point is that he was prepared to do so, though Allah may not actually require it.

We discussed various other topics, including the difficult question of the number of wives for a Muslim. Here, there was a slight disagreement. Zaheer asserted that the first wife must give permission for more wives; Iqbal gently and gracefully demurred, saying that no wife would give such permission. Zaheer deferred to superior authority!

24 May 1984: Group meeting in my secretary's flat. Since I came to Queen's, she has married a student, been confirmed, done courses on various faiths at the Multi-Faith Unit at Selly Oak Colleges and become a very regular member of our group. Not a requirement for continuing as my secretary! I went round to collect people, and went to the rich house where Iqbal has now taken over Zaheer's "duty", as he calls it. I rang the bell, and the children looked through the door. They ran in shouting excitedly, "Andrew has come!" I was moved. Nazir was with me and seemed hesitant about going in, since he has never been in such a house before. Iqbal brought along his special copy of the Qur'an this evening, engraved, from Iraq, wrapped in a coloured cloth cover, and this had to be carried into the meeting first; he said that he was bringing it as a sign of his recognition of spiritual qualities in some of us! Coming from him it is all the more touching, in view of his conservatism. Nazir told me again this evening that it is surprising we have kept him with us, because his origins are in an extreme sect. What was also good this evening was that we had a number of people from outside the college. This is broadening our base.

We began by discussing an article brought along by one of the Christians, from the Birmingham *Evening Mail*, heavily critical of Muslim evening classes for children. He said that it represented Western educational assumptions, but had no understanding of other cultural and religious backgrounds. We considered whether we should write a combined reply to the article.

We then passed to the main topic of the evening, which was in the area of ethics. We took texts from the Qur'an and parts of Matthew 5 and Matthew 25. Discussion was somewhat disjointed; our friends asked if they could go and say prayers, at the scheduled time, and they went off to a neighbouring flat. It was good that they felt able to ask to do this. We discussed Zakat offering, which was given only to Muslims, but there were other offerings to those in need generally. Another question raised was related to freedom. Iqbal was of the opinion that no force should be used to convert others, particularly Christians — and never has been used in Muslim history. But he was not happy with impressionable youth being allowed to go to see worship, for example, in Sikh gurdwaras. But, predictably, Nazir said he would allow such freedom since they would come back in the end. It is the sort of freedom he would give to his children. On the whole the Christians agreed with him.

We ended with prayers by a South Indian Christian colleague of mine who was with us; he spoke, too, of his experiences in dialogue. This was followed by a prayer from Iqbal, and then, spontaneously, by Zaheer for my secretary and her husband as they leave shortly. He prays so appropriately; he is better than most of our theological students at extempore prayer, and his prayers are marked by beauty of language and sensitivity.

27 June 1984: We went to Nazir's house for Iftar, the breaking of the fast at the end of a Ramadan day, which this year is at about 9.30 p.m. A magnificent spread — lettuce, oranges, melon, mango, bajis, meat and vegetable curry, and payasam. I was reminded of an experience in Pakistan, when the bus in which I was travelling between Lahore and Rawalpindi stopped at this time, and everyone shared their goodies.

We met Nazir's sister-in-law from Karachi, who had a lot to say for herself. Nazir explained that she is a "townie", not a country girl like his wife who is very shy. We prayed together before the meal, and then had what Nazir himself called a "good dialogue". I found myself answering a number of his questions about Hinduism. It struck me, not for the first time, that as Christians, if we can gain the trust of both, we could perform a useful role in promoting contacts and understanding between Hindus and Muslims with all their historical and theological divisions. The more I see of Pakistani Muslims, the more I sense the general influence of the culture of the sub-continent, which they share anyway with Hindus. Nazir told the story of how Allah sent the angel Gabriel to search for a pious man in a certain place. Gabriel saw a man praying before an idol, lying prostrate. He reported back to Allah that he could find only an idol worshipper. He was asked to go and look again. This time he heard the idol speak, saying: "I forgive you your sins, go in peace." He returned and told Allah the curious story, and Allah replied: "That was not really the idol speaking my word, that was me!" Where this comes from I do not know, but it is a very surprising story for a Muslim to tell, considering the normal attitude to idol-worship.

14 July 1984: At Zaheer's I met a young West Indian convert to Islam, and I asked him about his conversion.

"I converted only a week ago, and have taken a Muslim name — previously I was 'Vern'! Now I am Ibrahim."

"And what did your family think?" "I have a white mother and a West Indian father. I attended an Anglican church for a number of years. My family is angry with me, but has not used violence to stop me."

"What did you feel about God when you were a Christian?" "I didn't bother about him, and no-one else around me seemed to be bothered. But now I feel I am among people who take God seriously. I am very impressed by the way of life of the Muslim community, and the discipline involved."

He then spoke on the teaching he had been given, but argued it strongly: "The Qur'an is the truth, while the Bible is corrupt;

the Old Testament envisaged two prophets who were to come, one on an ass and the other on a camel, and this latter (Muhammad) is to be more accepted. And Jesus and the Old Testament agree about circumcision, with Islam, but St Paul had set this aside."

"What of the cross and resurrection of Jesus?" "Oh, I believed in these when I was a Christian, but they are not necessary; indeed, they are a sign of lack of faith, for God can raise us up directly."

This young man is one of several converts we have come into contact with, black and white, and all are very well trained. On the whole the blacks are much warmer towards us; the white converts have an aggressiveness that prevents any real dialogue. I think of another young black convert I met in the Central Mosque. He had come from the West Indies with his mother, and they had felt rejected in the main-line church; she had been led to a black-led Pentecostal church, but he did not like it and fell into "bad habits", as he put it, and then into despair. He was befriended by some Asian Muslims, and introduced to the fellowship of the mosque, and through this, he said, he had been able to discover his real identity, that he had been born a Muslim as all of us are, but had been made into a Christian by his parents. He had now found a religion that was very sustaining, and had changed his style of life.

31 October 1984: Contact has continued for me and one or two others through the summer. We have the problem, our group largely comprising students, that there is no continuity over the vacation. Also, a good number of them leave for near or distant parts of the country after they complete their studies. I must see this as an opportunity to spread the influence of our group more widely, so that, with the confidence of being involved here, they can attempt things on their own, with Muslims or people of other faiths. But this means expecting a readiness amongst our Muslim friends to make new relationships, and to cover some old ground with some new people as well. So I was a little anxious about our first meeting of the new year this evening. However, I was able to meet Zaheer beforehand and express this anxiety. In his inimitable way he said there was nothing to worry about, and actually made me feel that new people were a challenge.

This first meeting was at the Centre opened in March. It is now becoming also a training school for future Imams, and we were introduced to half a dozen boys in their middle teens, from different parts of the country, sent by their families to live here, attending the local school and then undergoing further training in the evening. A headmaster for the evening school has been brought from Pakistan, and the enthusiasm of all for the project will, I expect, compensate for the as yet rudimentary facilities that they have to put up with. At our meeting were about a dozen students, six old and six new, of different ages and backgrounds, women and men. There were five Muslims, apart from those at the centre — the old trinity and two others. One of them is Sadiq, whom I have met through Zaheer, a warm person, with a great sense of humour. He has a broad Birmingham accent, and asks pointed and penetrating questions. The other is Abbas, who is a magistrate, a local politician, and secular in a very sharp way. As we introduced ourselves, Iqbal was splendid in the way he asked each student follow-up questions about their background and experience.

In discussion, Iqbal tended to be at his most dogmatic; I suppose he felt he must fly the flag with a number of new people there. This extended even to the approval of the cutting off of the hands of thieves (I cannot remember how we came on to the topic, but Abbas demurred equally vigorously). The evening for me was overshadowed by the news of the murder of Indira Gandhi. At the end of the evening, Zaheer prayed for India spontaneously, in his usual sensitive way. Iqbal could not restrain himself, however, and as we drank tea afterwards said that, in his opinion, she had it coming to her! I found this hard at this particular moment, with India in confusion and needing all our prayers. Forgiveness is so much at the heart of the revelation of the nature of God as seen in Christ.

14 November 1984: An informal meeting at Zaheer's house — five friends in the front room and, as is so often the case, the children coming and going from the back room where the women remain. If I come when Zaheer is not there, they will invite me in, and I have a talk with his wife and mother. But if he is there, they say little, and usually only send in the tea. One of the men present today is an old sage of a figure, with a striking red beard. He speaks little or no English, but repeated a long story to Zaheer, translated for me, about a particular miracle he had witnessed in Pakistan on a recent visit. Zaheer clearly defers to him, because of his age and wisdom.

He said at one point: "I am here in the body, but feel also that I am in heaven at the same time — almost that I have already passed from death to life. I do not fear physical death at all." Iqbal was there, and this led him on to his favourite subject of heaven and hell: "I also think there is something to be said for the idea of purgatory. But this can only lessen the amount of punishment due, it cannot give a completely new chance."

He and Zaheer had recently conducted the wedding of a white Muslim and a Jewish girl. They said that she did not know much, and they had to reassure her greatly, and much support would be needed — Zaheer again as the pastor!

I had left my car lights on, and it wouldn't start. No problem, he said, and called a white neighbour to look at it — they were clearly very friendly. No success, and so most of the street joined in pushing it round to the garage. As we waited for a quick battery charge, discussion continued, this time about love.

There had been a film on television the previous evening about the Taj Mahal; about Shah Jahan's overwhelming love for Mumtaz, of how, upon her death, his hair had gone white in a week, after a life-time during which he had never been more than a room apart from her. When imprisoned later, he had erected a special mirror so that he could always see the Taj, which he had built as her memorial.

Iqbal exclaimed: "I cannot understand all this, it was such a waste and out of proportion." I said: "There was a woman who poured ointment over Jesus' feet, very costly ointment. Those looking on spoke just as you, Iqbal. But Jesus commended her for the great love that she had shown."

Zaheer predictably commented: "Love is central and abiding, and without it nothing is of worth. I understand what Jesus was saying." And then the car was ready!

I met Iqbal again in the evening, in his house. He always supplies us with the Qur'an passages to look at, for our next meeting. He again talked of Hinduism and wondered how there could be anything good in it. I spoke of a particular Hindu friend whom he might meet, and he agreed to. But he does find anything outside "the religions of the book" so very difficult. He told a Hadith, about the Prophet adjudicating in a land dispute about a well, and deciding in favour of a Jew against a Muslim.

19 November 1984: Went again to Sparkbrook Mosque with a dozen students. The usual open welcome. In discussion afterwards, they said that they do not feel the need to evangelize, since they have their work cut out to keep their own people. But in this, unemployment (about 40 percent in this area) is an ally, and actually helps people to pray — an interesting approach! Talk again of other faiths; they get on well with Hindus and Sikhs in the area, but they feel their religions are man-made, and not religions of revelation. They share the Indian culture with them, and this is where arranged marriages, and the use of music, as in Quwali, at the tombs of saints, come from. But neither is of the essence of Islam. They are saddened, too, by divisions within the community, both locally, and also between Iran and Iraq. But these divisions do not touch the essence of the faith and practice, which is the same throughout the world.

3 December 1984: Meeting in a student's flat, where we were asked as Christians to speak of how we saw the prophet Muhammad. This was important for us to have to do, and we began with two prepared responses. For often we look at the place of Christ in the two faiths, and this is easier in one way, because he has a clear place in the Muslim faith. This is always salutary for Christians to hear, since so often we feel that we own him. But this honouring of Jesus is not normally balanced by a serious reckoning with Muhammad. And when we find it difficult to hear Muslims saying that Muhammad is the last prophet, and so his words are central as the word of God, so setting aside the words of the gospel, we forget we do exactly this to a Muslim, as we see Christ as the final and complete revelation. We were now being asked: is he a prophet or not? I suppose we gave differing answers. But it is important that we had to face the question.

Discussion centred after some time around the idea of Jihad, and whether a prophet can fight a war, even a holy war for the preservation of faith. Here the stark difference between Jesus and Muhammad was seen to lie — and the cross therefore becomes inevitably the stumbling block, not only to Jews and Greeks, but also to Muslims.

7 February 1985: A big meeting at Zaheer's house, the first time we have had the whole group there. I think he felt a little embarrassed by the humbleness of his house, and the hospitality he could give. There was no need for him to worry. He invited, too, the local Imam, who has little English and needed translation, but whom Zaheer, with his natural humility, brought into things quite regularly, as an authority who should have his chance. The Imam had a real presence about him, and at the end he embraced me warmly, invited us to his mosque, and said he felt there were three of the students, apart from myself, who had a special calling in this direction of dialogue. He chose the ones I would have chosen, even though they had not necessarily spoken the most.

The topic of the evening was the place of Abraham in our two faiths, and we read passages from the Qur'an, and Iqbal from the Old Testament. The others find it difficult to prepare in advance, and only react to what he says. We pin-pointed a key difference, that Abraham in Islam is recognized as achieving his end, and dies at Mecca; this is not so in the Old Testament. I also read the passage from the Epistle to the Hebrews, that he died only seeing things from afar, and that is our picture of him. This they saw as a sign of the superiority of their tradition — that God would not allow his prophet to fail. But, nevertheless, the sense of unity was strong, and we expressed the hope that we might be able to have some Jewish involvement in a future meeting.

We had with us this evening a very articulate young Muslim, confident and orthodox. He had been at the last meeting too. He suddenly said: "What is the purpose of these meetings? My wish is to convert you, and that is what it should be about."

Zaheer said, with disarming simplicity: "It is about mutual understanding and friendship, and I have learnt so much over this last year or so."

One of our students said: "It has enabled me to see how much there is in common, and also to face honestly the points of difference, and not to suggest we are all the same."

I added: "In our increasingly divided society, our meetings are small signs of what is possible if we have the courage to cross our cultural and religious barriers. I believe they have been converting for a number of us from both faiths, including myself, but not in the sense that our brother meant. For me personally, I feel I have had a special privilege of having got to know as friends three men who are so different from each other, but who walk closely with the one God, in whose name we meet, with our differences. I have no doubt about that, and that is why praying together has become a part of our meetings; it is a natural recognition of this."

This time, I asked an evangelical student to pray, and I was surprised and delighted that he agreed. Whatever his motive in first coming to the meetings, he, too, could feel this was right.

20 July 1985: Our meetings have continued through the year, and now we face again the break for the long vacation, and the prospect of new students again. It does take considerable energy to maintain momentum! Today helped, however. I went with two who were still around, and with a German visitor and an Indian Christian couple, to a big festival to celebrate the death of the original saint in Pakistan who inspires those who follow his Sheikh here. There was a procession from Small Heath park to the Central Mosque, about three miles, with several thousand people. We came in at the tail end of this, and heard the speeches from the steps of the mosque, with the Sheikh in the centre in his resplendent green. Emphasis was on spiritual renewal and solidarity, and also on contributing to society here. The atmosphere was festive, with stalls all around selling books and tapes and clothes. We joined them at the meal which is always provided for all on these occasions. The two women in our party had to go upstairs with the Muslim women, which they did not find particularly easy, since no one around them spoke English. We found Zaheer serving the meals, with Nazir and many others — it is a duty he loves, and doing this humdrum task is typical of him. He was delighted we were there. On a visit at an earlier function, he had taken me aside to a room in the mosque for an informal and impromptu dialogue meeting, which had been vigorous and ended, to my astonishment, with his asking me to pray with another of the brothers. In the Central Mosque! On this occasion, however, he was too busy serving, and so he guided us upstairs to listen to the speeches, which we did for a time before sharing in the tea.

11 September 1985: I was visiting someone in a peaceful residential area when we heard the news that Handsworth, just four miles away, was in flames. There was a feeling of unreality about it, as it seemed to have happened without provocation. But all the conditions were there for what is seen as a riot, or disturbance, or insurrection, depending from whose viewpoint you speak. It was of course not the whole of Handsworth but one street, Lozells Road, but that was tragic enough. Zaheer lives on one of the side streets off that road. And so my first thoughts were of him and his family, and I went to see them today, two days after the troubles.

I found him quite shattered by it all. His wife was out and came back while I was there; she had been with a vanload of Muslim women, to console the family of the two Asian Post Office workers killed in the blaze. Zaheer explained that they were friends with all the communities there, and he just could not understand what had come upon them. He has always said that the three communities, white, Asian and Afro-Caribbean, get along perfectly well in the side streets where he lives, and everything I have seen through him would indicate this. They had all been very very frightened, he said, and did not know what had happened. He was clear, however, that he did not feel it was local black people who were to blame — they were as shocked as anyone else — but that it was mainly those from outside, as well as the conditions that left unemployed youth, of whatever race, hanging around the street. As I would have expected of him, there was no bitterness. This made it all the sadder when I read some of the media coverage of it as a racial rather than social question, in order to divert attention from the basic conditions in which people live in the area, particularly those of chronic under-investment in housing and unemployment in all ages and communities, especially among the youth.

These things we discussed; by now two or three others had joined us, and Zaheer asked me to pray for them and the area, which I did, feeling it was something he really valued. We then walked up Lozells Road, smouldering in the aftermath. We took with us Zaheer's daughter, who walked between us, hand in hand. People were hanging around the streets, of all races, including some with Rastafarian haircuts. There was a feeling of tension; but also it struck me that even today people were talking to each other, in a way that does not often happen in the so-called desirable residential areas.

30 October 1985: At Zaheer's suggestion, we held a meeting in his local mosque in Lozells. It was a damp evening, but there was a good attendance. Our group included a number of new students, and a Brahmin Hindu from Madras. We also had a West Indian student with us and an old West Indian Muslim named Abbas was there. There were perhaps a dozen Muslims all told, including the Imam, and about fifteen Christians.

We began by witnessing the regular prayers. What was helpful for the new students was that the Imam went through the actions first, and explained them to them, and allowed questions about prayer, before the official prayers began. We then had tea, in small groups, served in the prayer hall itself, and it was on the basis of this relaxed start that we moved on to reflect about the recent happenings in the area, in the light of our respective religious traditions. Zaheer began, and spoke of the experience they had gone through. He added how he believed that this was a challenge for the communities and faiths to work together for a new future; but his own gentleness prevents him really from facing the hard political and social issues. The old West Indian Muslim then spoke. At his age, he said, you live on the frontier between life and death, and this is something he is no longer afraid of. He had been asleep when things had got out of hand, and as he woke, he thought he had passed over that frontier, to such a strange world had he come. The lesson for him is that we must always be ready to make that journey, since it may come to any of us at any time. And Allah will then receive us. I later learnt how much he is permeated by both his old Christian faith, and his new Muslim faith; none of us are logical people, and the sharpness of the differences seem in his case not to be exclusive but inclusive, and his spirit to drink from both wells.

He is rooted in the Bible, and he nodded his head vigorously when our next contributor, a young and highly political theological student, read a number of passages from the Gospels, including the parable of the rich fool. He expounded the story of how the rich man built barns and there was no room for more, and so he built more, ready to store the bumper harvest; and then he died that night. He interpreted this as a lesson to the white, largely nominal Christian community. They live in their comfy suburbs, and mutter about what happens in Handsworth. They make their money at the expense of the poor, and then wonder when it all goes up in flames. The whole incident is a call to us white Christians to repent and begin again. Quite a message to be heard in a mosque. This was followed by the young West Indian Christian student sharpening the debate, saying that we have to face the conflict and the political and economic questions involved, and we cannot hide behind the spiritualizing of it all.

One or two of the Muslims took this up vigorously, especially a newcomer, Qazi, whom we were to get to know well in the next months. He is a grandfather, in his sixties, and clearly respected as a senior figure in the community. He told us later that he comes from Gujarat, in India, from a family of considerable standing; as a youth he had met a number of leading Indian politicians, including Dr Ambedkar, who founded the Siddarth College in Bombay where Qazi studied. Dr Ambedkar was the leading politician from the "untouchable" community who became a Buddhist in the 1950s, along with several thousand fellow "untouchables". He is revered today as a great leader and founder of the neo-Buddhist movement. Qazi has great capacity for sympathy. He gave an impressive speech, combining political practicalities — he is active in this area — with the resources of his faith, and he quoted extensively from the Qur'an, seeking wisdom for a situation that called for justice and reconciliation.

Airing of views continued, and though nothing concrete was planned, the very meeting itself was a sign that what we bring from our respective faiths is a common commitment to the same community goals and aims, the Christians on the whole coming from those who hold power, the Muslims from those who are powerless. And from where we stand in this equation is determined the sort of action that is required. I came away thinking how we might work together for common goals, on the basis of the friendship we have built up. And we are seen to have power

— I was in Zaheer's house recently, when a friend of his came and out of the blue asked me to write a letter supporting plans he was submitting for change of the use of a house into a house mosque. I think, too, of the issue of the broadcasting of the call to prayer at the Central Mosque, and how the secretary has been very anxious to gain my support and that of other Christians, since we are assumed to have influence.

We had prayers, and after Qazi had been asked to pray I was asked too. What a privilege, to be asked to pray, as a Christian priest, in a mosque in Lozells, publicly, for peace and justice in the area. I think the Spirit helped me to find the right words, and people were drawn together, and not apart, by both the prayers. Nazir then asked us all to sign a petition he had drawn up, about doctors charging too high fees for doing the circumcision operation required for a Muslim boy, and demanding that this should be done on the National Health system, because it is a cultural necessity. We gladly did so.

2 November 1985: I had gone to tell Zaheer about the illness of my brother-in-law Khalid. He has had rheumatic pains for some time, and has been off work. He now faces a major operation to investigate a shadow on his lung. I naturally asked him to be prayed for in our college chapel and, equally naturally for me now, told Zaheer, and he offered to pray for him, which he did with great conviction. He then told me to come back today, because he wished to take me to his Sheikh, so that he also could offer prayer. And so we went off to Sparkbrook, and waited for audience with the great man, in his house converted into reception room and prayer house. We were shown in, and I felt the same as when I had visited a Hindu holy man on one or two occasions in India. Zaheer was very submissive in his manner, and explained who I was and what the problem was. I was then asked to go through it in my own words. The Sheikh gave some words of encouragement for Khalid, which I was to pass on, and said he would now pray for him. This he did at great length, for ten minutes or so, and at the same time, he took some yellow wool, several strands together, and made knots in it, at intervals of a few inches, after each sequence of prayers. He gave this to me, and Zaheer explained that I should send it to Khalid, who was then to wear it during his operation. The

Sheikh then wrote out a *tawiz* — a verse of Qur'an, which Khalid was to wear round his neck. He also gave a bundle of small, ready-made verses, on small pieces of paper, which he should take in water, one each day. I thanked him, and we left.

Zaheer was clearly delighted at what had happened. He had given, through the Sheikh, what he felt was the best he could for Khalid. I felt strangely at ease with the whole thing. The *tawiz* and the wool were symbols of the offer of real prayer for healing, from the best of the Sufi tradition, for a fellow Muslim. I found the swallowing of the paper, like medicine, rather less easy, but this was a minor point, compared with the whole feeling of care and prayer that surrounded the visit. And if it is God who heals, is their God who heals different from my God, revealed in Jesus as the God of healing?

18 November 1985: There is good news from Khalid. He has had the operation, and they have not found anything untoward. He did wear the wool during the operation, explaining to the doctor that it had been given to him by his priest brother-in-law! He feels both physically and spiritually revived by the time in hospital, and says he found himself next to a professor from the local university, who had no particular beliefs and to whom he had found himself witnessing! (Not something he would normally have done before.) I went over to tell Zaheer who rejoiced. I told him, too, of all the Christian prayers that had been said, and we smiled, and agreed that they had reinforced each other!

11 December 1985: I myself have been ill with a virus infection which has given me strong headaches. I missed our last meeting, when Zaheer spoke about his visit to Mecca on Haj pilgrimage. He had achieved his life's ambition, which was not just to go but to take his mother.

Today, Zaheer and Qazi and Sadiq came to our college Advent carol service. It was good to have them there, and also at the party held afterwards. I warned them that there alcoholic punch would be served, as well as coffee. They did not mind, as long as they did not have to consume it. They felt, I think, quite at home. I was still suffering from the headaches, and Zaheer took me out from the party, and said he wanted to pray for me, and laid hands very firmly on my temples as he spoke. He ended his prayer by blowing three times over my head, which he said is a Sufi way of releasing a healing power. His prayer was not in English, and as he prayed I prayed in my mind, as a Christian, for healing for myself and for others I knew. Hardly what normally happens in a theological college. And again it seemed entirely right and natural, on the basis of our friendship and trust, though many would find this, in the abstract, difficult to accept.

23 January 1986: We met as a group in Qazi's house. He has a house on one side of the road, where he lives, and this other house on the opposite side, which he uses for prayer and study, and to receive visitors and have such meetings. We crowded into the small room, about twenty of us in all. The topic of the evening was to compare the Franciscan way of life and teaching with that of a Sufi order. A Franciscan brother from the college is now part of the group and, wearing his habit, he held all of us spellbound with a simple but profound account of the calling of St Francis, his life and teaching, and of his own response to this. The message seemed to speak quite beyond the bounds of one religion. We then heard an exposition of what being a Sufi was about from Nazir's own brother — and he suggested that this was no more and no less than what being a truly spiritual Muslim was about. We felt the same, too, about the example of St Francis, who was doing no more and no less than calling the church back to the true gospel of Christ. There was one dissenter among the Muslims, Farooq, a reporter from a Muslim paper, who later wrote an article on the meeting, and has come regularly since and been positive. But at this stage he was clearly testing out the ground, was out of sympathy with some of the ideas coming from the Sufi tradition, and wanted to say what the true Islamic faith says. However, he did not prevent people from speaking from the heart, and it continued as a searching evening.

We moved on to the whole question of poverty, and our response. We have also now, as part of the group, a Roman Catholic priest, and he questioned the idea of personal charity which so often satisfies Christians. St Francis was actually challenging a whole system with his revolutionary style of life, and that is what we may have to do. In this light, we considered whether institutionalized Zakat is enough for a Muslim, and opinions varied.

We adjourned then for food and prayer, and all Qazi's family came in, his wife and son and daughter and daughter-in-law and grandchildren. It was now about 11 o'clock at night, and a number of us remained behind for this family dialogue! The greater freedom we see here is a result, I think, of his Indian, rather than Pakistani background.

15 February 1986: Qazi called me round, and asked me to mobilize my students in joint support with him of the Rev. Richard Rogers. Richard is to spend the whole of Lent shut in a cage in St Martin's Church in central Birmingham, to draw attention to the plight of a Christian poet, Irina Ratushinskaya, imprisoned in the Soviet Union. Qazi had met him when being treated in hospital — Richard is also a surgeon. I was impressed with Qazi's breadth of sympathy. The campaign in general is to be for the cause of all religious prisoners in the Soviet Union, and these include, of course, Christians, Jews and Muslims. Qazi himself is moved by the particular plight of Irina, and it matters nothing to him that she is a Christian. Later a Muslim prisoner was also added for special focus, but his support was by no means conditional on this. And he entered into the support with great vigour, personally sending letters to over a hundred mosques, requesting special prayers, and also to the Soviet Embassy and about a hundred other embassies. He asked for our help — I was pleased that it should be this way round, not us asking him, and I said I would go and meet Richard, with some of our group, and decide how we should proceed.

29 March 1986: Convinced of the sensitivity of Richard's campaign, and urged on by Qazi, we from the college helped in various ways. Today we expressed this multi-faith aspect of a common concern for human rights by holding a joint witness in St Martin's on Holy Saturday. We had hoped to get Jewish participation, but as it was the Sabbath that was not possible. Jews and Muslims would have found it hard to be together anyway. One of the Muslims found the idea of Jewish involvement difficult; he was full of hatred for the Jews. He was a recent convert, a West Indian, and I found myself arguing with him rather emotionally. Qazi was superb and calmed the situation; he explained to me afterwards that the spirit of true Islam had not yet penetrated, and wanted me to forgive him. A ministry of reconciliation!

The rector of St Martin's gave us every help, and on the busy Saturday afternoon some 50 Christians and about 12 Muslims gathered round Richard's "cage", at the back of the church. To my surprise, the Muslims began by asking if they could do their regular prayers in the church, and offer "Dua" for the cause concerned. The rector said he was happy for them to do this, and they looked round for a suitable place; they chose, in the end, the side chapel where there was the Easter garden! Here they rolled out their prayer mats, and Qazi led them in their prayers, facing Mecca, as the rest of us stood round in silent witness.

We then proceeded to the planned part of the service, of which I felt quite nervous. It somehow seemed a big step to take into a public situation what had been very much a gathering of friends. When the Muslims were praying, I was praying myself with a Jewish Christian friend, and this calmed me considerably. The rector began by welcoming us, and I then introduced the service, and said quite clearly that the idea was not to force anything on anyone, and that for some what they would do would be to pray the parts which they could pray, led by members of their own faith, and quietly witness as those of other faiths prayed. For others, who had spent much time together, it might be possible to pray each other's prayers. We should all do what we were happy and comfortable with, and each witness in our own way to the common cause of human rights, not just in the Soviet Union, but wherever injustice might reign and individuals suffered, of whatever faith. And so much had happened between our faiths in history that it was good that we could come together like this on a common cause.

Qazi then began things from the Muslim side, giving an exposition of parts of the Qur'an and their bearing on human rights, and calling on us to unite in prayer for those who are poor and oppressed. He then recited three suras from the Qur'an, including, from Sura 11.286, the words: "O Lord, condemn us not if we forget or fall into error; O Lord, lay not on us a burden greater than we have the strength to bear. Blot out our sins, and grant us forgiveness. Have mercy on us, Thou art our protector. Help us against those who stand against faith." I then spoke a little about human rights and the gospel, and we had a series of readings: from Amos, by the Jewish Christian who was present, and then from Matthew 25, and, to widen the perspective, from Allan Boesak. This flowed naturally into the singing of St Francis' prayer: "Lord, make me an instrument of thy peace..." I had checked that the Muslims would be happy with this, knowing their feelings about music in worship. They were, and indeed some of them joined in.

We turned round then to the cage, and Richard spoke to us, on this last day of his "sentence", appreciating this joint-faith support. We then read one of Irina's poems, about her husband whom she now can never see, and led from this into free prayer. I prayed, and then the Roman Catholic priest from Handsworth who was present. He is Irish, and he prayed in an unambiguously Christian way, through Jesus Christ our Lord. No one minded this, as the framework of freedom to pray as we will had already been set, and he prayed with such warmth (and not to make a theological point, as sometimes happens on such occasions!). I then asked Zaheer to pray, but he said no, give a chance to the old West Indian Muslim because, Zaheer said with a twinkle in his eye, "he is a Muslim Christian". And truly in some sense he is, since he prayed very much as a Christian from the West Indies would, and drew us all together. The rector then gave an appropriate blessing and, not having planned it beforehand, out of the blue I suggested that we hold hands and sing together Shalom, led by the Jewish friend. It was a gamble, but I think it worked. An appropriate comment on the whole act of witness.

1 May 1986: We met at the community centre, to discuss the place of festivals and fasting in our two faiths. We began by being shown round the new printing press they have there. This do-it-yourself approach reminds me of the small printing presses which have sprung up everywhere in India. Our discussion was timed for this evening, as Ramadan begins next week. One of us spoke about the practice of Lent, and made as much as he could of it. But it seemed a puny thing to offer, particularly as the Muslims emphasized very clearly that the discipline of fasting was not an end in itself, but was to be complemented by extra prayer and devotion, and also by the doing of extra good deeds. Moreover, the fasting was so much part of their way of life, and such a healthy thing, that they were happy to do extra days at the end. And the especially devout could sit in a mosque, and spend the last few days in quiet, behind a sheet, reading the Qur'an from end to end. Each mosque should be so blessed, and one of our friends was to go to a small house mosque, since they had none available. And all this without legalism; if you cannot manage it some days, then you can do it at some later time in the year.

5 June 1986: We were invited by Qazi and his family to join them for Iftar, on one of the days of the Ramadan. We decided to join in the fasting on that day which was from 2 a.m. until 9.30 p.m. I was told by Qazi that as I had a busy day, I should take liquids, but one or two of the others decided to do the full fast.

Through this experience we felt in a new way the joy and celebration of Iftar as the sun sank behind the tower blocks of Central Birmingham. We broke the fast in traditional fashion, by eating dates and sweetmeats, which were all laid out for us. We adjourned to the back room to witness the prayers, where special intention was made for us. We returned then to the front room for a magnificent meal, with Qazi acting very much in the role of "pater familias", and beaming with pleasure in the occasion. He told us story after story from India, several from Hindu sources, and then asked for our stories, including Irish ones, because our Roman Catholic priest was with us. Islam may appear sombre to some and clearly there is that side — but we really did feel we had been to a party on this occasion.

11 June 1986: Our last formal meeting of the year, at Queen's. It was both a sad and joyous occasion as we said good-bye to friends. The Muslims began asking questions about the work of leavers; we got into discussing all the differences between the Methodist minister, the Anglican curate, and a Roman Catholic priest, since we had all three with us, and to complicate things further an Anglican woman deacon! We had an interesting comparison, too, with the different people who might provide such functions within the Muslim community. They also passed on suggestions about contacts with Muslims the leavers could make, in the places they were going to. And so Zaheer gathered in prayer together all those who were leaving, by name, and there was a real sending out.

At the end, our young West Indian student made an announcement about the celebration of Soweto Day on the following Monday, which this year is to be a time of prayer and fasting of special intention, because it is the tenth anniversary of the massacre there, and also comes at a crucial stage in the Emergency clampdown in South Africa. Qazi proposed that the Muslims join us in this, and we made plans for another joint witness, this time in Queen's Chapel, the evening of this day, after fasting. The Muslims said that they would fast as for a day of Ramadan, from dawn to dusk. And so we agreed to meet at 9.30 p.m. on Monday.

16 June 1986: It was a beautiful summer evening, which somehow only seemed to heighten the sense of anguish for South Africa, which is going through such traumas at the moment. About eight or nine Muslims came, and there were some thirty Christians from the College community and one or two from outside. We began by breaking the fast together, with fruits offered from both communities, which was almost sacramental in the way it symbolized the unity of the gathering. The Muslims then said their night prayers, facing Mecca. There was a short debate as to whether they should say them in the chapel, in front of the crucifix, or outside on the lawn. We were happy for them to make use of the chapel, if they did not mind the crucifix, which clearly would not and should not be removed. They decided to go ahead and seemed happy with this. They made special "Dua" for South Africa, while the Christians there remained in silent meditation and prayer. I felt glad to see the college principal there, showing his appreciation of our work in public. We had his encouragement all the time, but this was a different matter. I wonder when, if ever, such a thing had happened in a British theological college chapel.

The lead was then taken by our West Indian student who explained the purpose of the gathering, and how each should pray as his or her conscience permitted. Qazi also got up and said that it was not just Christians who were involved in South Africa; he said he had been visited that very week by an Indian friend who had come out of South Africa as an exile, because he could no longer live there. Since Gandhi had begun the struggle, Indians had been involved, and particularly so again in the present. There followed then a series of readings, and the playing of a tape of music, and the singing of a hymn. All happened at a gentle pace, and we seemed to meet in the silence in between, as we lifted up in prayer our brothers and sisters in South Africa. We ended with extempore prayer, and in this both Zaheer and Qazi joined. This was followed by tea and more sharing of fruits and biscuits, and also the signing of a petition recording our joint faith call for a new beginning in South Africa.

A postscript to the diary

There have been many ups and downs during our journey. Some because of simple practicalities, just the trouble of keeping things going, with the nagging question, is it all worth it? There is the suspicion from the Christian end that you are misleading students of the ministry into thinking that involvement with Islam or Hinduism is more important than understanding their own faith better, when they have so much to learn there. The time for training is short, and students should not be diverted in this way. Our critics choose not to notice that the group is entirely voluntary, and does encourage students to understand their own faith better. There are other Christians who do not say it, but imply that you are betraying the essence of the faith; that you are suggesting, which you are not, that all roads lead to God, and that such relativism is a betrayal of Jesus Christ.

Then from the Muslim end you have a sense sometimes that you have been together for a long time, but in the end you often seem to be back at the beginning, with the same stumbling blocks, and the same difficulty in relating to scripture and authority, and to the centre points of our faiths. There are the moments of misunderstanding, and the points where a sharp red light is displayed. You are sure of mutual trust — and yet...

All this is to say that things did not come easily. The account given above highlights some of the important occasions. It tones down the struggles and disappointments, the times when we seemed to be speaking alongside but not to each other. In between, and even within these events, there was the toil, and occasionally the agony too. Even the agony, sometimes, of feeling the deep faith of these friends, and feeling something lacking in it, something that can only be found in responding to God in Christ.

In general there is the frustration of lack of time. This is just one of many things we do. Sometimes I think, if only I had nothing else to concentrate on, how much could be achieved! But then, is that not the reality for nearly all of us of whatever faith, whether we are lay or ordained? This is an example, then, of what can be done when one is not able to be a specialist. It is again realistic and right that only a proportion, which will vary from year to year, will be interested in this area. This again is a natural frustration for anyone who believes in something. We want all to accompany us, whether in college or parish. We learn to be glad that some do.

Different frustrations come in relating to different faiths. (And of course, different possibilities too.) With Islam, its very clarity becomes a frustration, as also its readily worked out response to Christian positions. With Hindus, we have found it easy to be involved in one-off and colourful occasions, be they festivals in a temple, or witnessing prayer to Sai Baba, the guru/avatar (incarnation) living in South India, but very popular here. What has been much more difficult is any sustained encounter, except with one particular highly educated Brahmin woman, with whom we have had regular discussion around the Bhagavad Gita. In general, learning about Hinduism is easy and enjoyable; but deeper discussion has ended up quickly at the point where they explain how they believe there are many ways to God, and the Christian way is a very acceptable one. With Sikhs at a religious level, we tend to end at the same place, but there is the added frustration of needing to relate closely to the politics of the Punjab with which overseas Sikhs are so much preoccupied.

The deepest frustration has been with our attempts to relate to the Jewish community. In Birmingham, the community is small and declining, through people marrying out, through emigration to Israel, and through the remaining people moving to larger Jewish communities within Britain. In this situation, and in view of the anguish of Jewish-Christian history, it is not surprising that it is difficult to move forward in friendship. There is, too, great suspicion about Christians having ulterior motives, particularly with the number of organizations around concerned directly with conversion of the Jews. To this general feeling was added in Birmingham the suicide of a Jewish convert to Christianity a few years ago and the bitter feeling this has left. We feel a real longing to get closer to a faith that is deep in our roots, not just for historical reasons, but to understand better the present-day Judaism around us. But we have not got far in this. To visit orthodox synagogues is not easy, which is an opportunity lost, in that students gain so much when they do go, which they can contribute to Jewish-Christian understanding in their future ministry. In meetings we have held, there have been memorable discussions about subjects like forgiveness, the Holocaust, and issues of contemporary Judaism. But at times we have felt we are treading on thin ice. And though a number may come to an occasion, suddenly most will not turn up the next time. You are left wondering what may have caused offence. It is probably nothing at all, and just busy programmes or miscommunication from our side. But Auschwitz lies between us, and nearly every family in Birmingham might have lost someone in the Holocaust, for many their whole families. This we understand, as far as anyone who is not a Jew can. But it remains sad for us that dialogue can be sustained with our Muslim friends, but not so far with local Jewish people, who are from the very rock of which we are hewn.

I acknowledge, too, that we have been very fortunate in the particular Muslims with whom we have become friends. There are many groups of Muslims in Birmingham with whom it would be impossible to have the type of relationship that we have with Zaheer and Nazir and Iqbal and Qazi and others. I am aware that we should not generalize from this situation to any other one, even within Britain. Others will have less happy stories to tell. But I believe this makes it all the more important to bring an example that is positive to this often rather depressing scene of Christian-Muslim relationships.

3. Reflections on the Encounter

Both the World Council of Churches and the British Council of Churches have brought out guidelines for dialogue. The British Council guidelines are based on the World Council document, working out in more detail, and in a way suitable to the British context, the principles set out by the world body. How we are to relate to people of other faiths will follow certain general principles which would be applicable wherever we are. Such principles will reflect our theological understandings and reckon with the requirements of the Christian gospel and its call to mission. They must also reflect contextual realities. I have dealt with some of the contextual realities in our situation. Here I would like to consider what we can learn of dialogue from this particular situation, and use the British Council of Churches' guidelines within that discussion. Readers from other places will make their own responses; it is the nature of contextual theology that its application will be different in different places. But my hope is that there will be things that can be of help more widely than in just the British context.

The first of the British Council principles of dialogue is that dialogue begins when people meet people. I will deal with these reflections around the common theme of "meeting". Without such meeting nothing can begin. The following sections will briefly take up the practicalities of meeting, meeting as persons, meeting as persons of faith, meeting as persons of prayer, theological reflection on meeting, and meeting in the Spirit. This of course is only for the sake of convenience. I am aware that experience is not divided like this; all these take place at the same time and, in the end, should be seen as a whole.

Practicalities of meeting

This is the least interesting in a sense, but crucial for any real encounter to get off the ground. A sense of freedom is needed as regards time and place. In the end we do not "control" things, and nor can a Western sense of time and order. The feeding of the five thousand took place when people had lost their sense of time as they remained spellbound listening to Jesus. Meetings strictly between 7.30 p.m. and 9 p.m., a typical time for church meetings, may not work, as we must allow for more flexibility. When unexpected opportunity arises, we may have to set aside the early night. And at the beginning, we may need to be patient, as people arrive from here and there at different times. We can "redeem the time" with those who have already come, while we wait for a formal start. Often the best parts of an evening are the unseen parts, when people talk in twos and threes before and after the more organized dialogue. It is at such times that we are really able to engage with a person of another faith and culture, while others lapse back into the safety of relaxing with the friend they have come with, and the opportunity passes them by.

Simple human qualities of perseverance and stability will take us a long way. To reach deeper levels of meeting and trust, we have to keep going, and it is not always easy. There will be frustrations and dry periods, when nothing much seems to be happening, or we are slipping backwards. Easy too to feel we are going over the same old ground. There will be the annoying journeys to houses when arrangements have to be made, only to find the door opened, not by the person we have gone to see but by some uncomprehending elderly relative who knows nothing of your existence or of the whereabouts of their son whom you are supposed to meet. You are invited in to what could easily be an indefinite wait. You say to yourself, well, at least I can use the time for getting to know the family, and some interesting talk may come up. But instead, you are put in the front room, served a cup of tea, and left totally alone. After half an hour, you leave, not having met your friend, and with nothing apparently accomplished.

There is the problem, too — very hard for Westerners — of dealing with those who are not on the telephone. This can be seen as a mere frustration. But even in normal Western life, how much real meeting is prevented by the telephone, as well as facilitated by it. You cannot in so many communities just drop in on a friend or neighbour. A telephone call must be made first. And often that call will complete the business, and it is not necessary to meet at all. To have to go round and call allows opportunity for informal meeting, and of such is the stuff of dialogue made, religious or otherwise. In the large Indian seminary I taught at, we had just one telephone. Everything, internal and external, had to be done by personal meeting. Tiring and frustrating in the heat. But there was opportunity for real meeting.

We may be expected to do things that are not easy for us. It is not easy for those who have always sat on chairs to have to sit on the floor, and for long periods. Taking off our shoes may make us feel uncomfortable and half dressed. It is difficult to eat food which is new to us, and which we may positively dislike, and sweet, scented tea may not be our cup of tea! It is also frustrating if we have prepared food for our visitors of another faith, and they refuse to eat, on impeccable religious grounds. We may feel easily that it's unfair; we eat what he presents, why does he not eat what we are giving out of our hospitality! It is easy to forget the basically different attitude to these things in the different faiths, and project on to, say, a Muslim, the view of freedom which we as Christians enjoy, which he sees perhaps as undisciplined licence. Respecting sensitivity is very important. How sad, and how hindering to the mission of the church, has been the way it has become almost a mark of becoming a proper Christian, in parts of India, to eat meat, and especially beef. We forget so easily the message of St Paul about respecting the conscience of others. He was referring to other members of the Christian community who found eating food offered to idols intolerable. But surely we can apply this to people of other faiths too. So let us find out what a particular Muslim, or group of Muslims, are prepared to eat, and offer the best of that. It is by no means the same with each Muslim, and we can be sensitive to this too. It is also not a restriction he wishes to impose on non-Muslims, it is a rule of life for themselves. I found this very clearly in Pakistan, when travelling during Ramadan. Muslims were most strict themselves — indeed, were required to be by the government — but also made sure that I was fed well, serving me meals at all the regular times.

Such acceptance has to apply also to the question of women and their participation in meetings. Unless we are involved with a very unrepresentative group of Muslims, such participation is likely to be nil. This is not easy for sensitive and articulate Christian women to accept. Why should they be there, and not their Muslim counterparts? The Muslims will not, in my experience, mind at all women taking part from the Christian side. But we will not help ourselves by projecting our view of what the women in the backroom or kitchen may feel about being "left out", as they prepare food for us. For many of them, it would be the height of embarrassment to be ushered into the front room, where their menfolk are so relaxed. This again points to the difference between our two faiths in this area. Added to this are cultural differences. Many Indian Christian women would not be happy to be part of such meetings. Differences in how women are seen, and how marriage takes place, can certainly be compared and faced up to. Great tensions are already felt among the new generation of Muslim young women as they are caught between cultures and between school and mosque. But in all this, we can suggest a cultural superiority about "our way" of doing things which is by no means obvious to the Muslim; in fact, quite the reverse, as he looks around at the results of what he sees as "Christian" freedom.

Another concern is the question of group dynamics, which is important in any meeting between more than two people, on whatever subject. One-to-one meetings between key people are necessary if group meetings are to be sustained. Our experience is that time given between meetings is crucial to the sustaining of the group. And there needs to be an overall and over-riding commitment from at least one member from each faith. For most of the group, interfaith meetings will be one of many things, to which they will come along without any deep commitment. Those who are more committed should not condemn them for this, but be glad that they feel they do come in the way they can. But those who are to be "leaders" in an official or unofficial way should not underestimate the time and energy involved, or become easily disappointed. And leadership must come from both sides, and be seen to do so. Most of this leadership will be behind the scenes and should not lead to domination at meetings. Here it is important to enable, and not take over or control. The meetings are of course best when there is roughly equal participation from both sides. Otherwise one or another of the smaller group becomes the spokesperson, and it becomes a question-and-answer session but not a real group experience. The problem is how long to allow one person to speak, and how to break in if it seems a never-ending sermon is being given.

It is usually good to have some people prepared to give a short introduction to discussions, but again, how to make sure this remains short is a regular challenge. It is important, too, that people should feel free to remain silent and listen, and not feel inferior if they do not speak. They need to feel it is okay to be there, and to be carefully listening; that itself is a contribution, when so often people are only too ready to talk. It is good also to be sensitive to the length of a meeting, in a formal way. There is a time when it is right to finish; and if this is still when people are interested, it is likely that they will not then rush off but engage in what is often the much more important personal contact, in informal ways over tea or refreshments. The group should be very open, with people free to come and go, either at any particular meeting, or from one meeting to another. It is not a question of attendance registers! The question of participation of leaders of religious communities is a delicate one. If they can be sensitive, this will be a benefit as they can add their particular expertise from their training. But too often in certain traditions, there is an inbuilt deference from lay people, and they will not speak freely in front of their official leader. With our Muslim friends we have found this sometimes; those who are articulate and wise in our experience feel they must say little or nothing in the presence of the Imam. And if the Imam does not speak English, he will have to be translated as he gives his official input. Often, too, he will speak with a greater authority, and dialogue becomes much more difficult; he is there to maintain orthodoxy. No doubt the same can and does happen with Christian clergy! But how they are to participate is an important part of considering the dynamic of the group.

Finally, and not least important, there is a need for a sense of humour. Over-earnestness can be disastrous. A shared sense of humour is a keymark of friendship. Just one example. Recently I was asked to a gathering to receive a noted Turkish Sheikh to Birmingham. I went with one of our students at the appointed hour, 8 p.m., to Nazir's house. He was dressed in his best Sufi clothes, as were the large number of his friends who had gathered. The women were preparing a great feast in the back room, and we talked in the front. A painted portrait of the Sheikh was produced, and we heard from Nazir a testimony to his spiritual power and saintly presence, such as he imagined was the case with Christ, Muhammad and the Buddha. Time went by and only at 10 p.m. did the great man appear, followed by a retinue from London, including a number of German Muslims. (Does a considerable turning to Sufism amongst some young Germans indicate a possible vacuum in spirituality in much of the cerebral and socially committed German Protestant Church?)

We sat around the Sheikh, and waited for his words of wisdom. What came was a tirade of irritation and anger at Nazir, who seemed to be completely unruffled. Zaheer, who was sitting next to me, smiled and muttered: "Nazir is getting a mouthful, because he did not send anyone to escort the Sheikh, who got lost in the back streets!"

We all then marched off to the mosque, where there were too many to have the prayers in one sitting, and many women also, who had to pray separately in relays. And so it was 11 p.m. before the meeting began. Yet it then switched gear into what was rather like a charismatic meeting, as the name of Allah was chanted, and eyes closed in concentrated meditation, as a preliminary to the Sheikh's sermon.

The important thing about the evening was not just that my student and I could smile together, but that Zaheer could join us. When I said we would have to go before midnight, he laughed and winked and said he had a bit of a headache too, and would have to make an excuse and go!

Meeting as persons

What is described at the beginning of the diary — 17 November 1983 — is a clear example of what happens when people do not meet people. There was no interest in each other as people, only in the comparing of systems. What must have seemed unlikely at the beginning is that such different groups as my students and myself from a theological college could begin and sustain a relationship with a group of working-class Muslims from a totally different culture. According to the British Council Guidelines: "What makes dialogue between us possible is our common humanity, created in the image of God. We all experience the joys and sorrows of human life, we are citizens of one country, we face the same problems, we all live in God's presence." This latter is important. We all acknowledge the relevance of God in our lives, which is surely not something now generally acknowledged in the wider society of Britain. This gives us a great common bond. So, too, we are struggling with questions of prayer and worship and ethics, and the injustices so obvious in our society.

On this basis and foundation, real friendship is possible across cultural and religious barriers. It is possible to become "brothers and sisters", if we really wish to be such. Such terms of course may be just an embarrassment to us, and so cannot have any real or reciprocal meaning. But it is possible to feel real warmth and symbolic depth of meaning in mutual embrace as we greet each other across all the human barriers. The person we meet ceases to be just Muslim X, or Hindu Y, and becomes Hussein or Patel, my friends. From both sides we must wish for such friendship, and really believe it possible, or we may always be on our guard. I am always struck by the way those who have had even one genuine and deep cross-cultural friendship with those of another culture or faith are half-way there in terms of all future types of friendships that we are describing. It may be with the Hindu doctor living next door, or with the Jewish family across the road. It may have little to do with religion at all; but such friendships give confidence.

On the other hand, the person who cannot make friendships outside his or her own class or group, even with people of the same culture, is very unlikely to be able to do this with those who are more obviously different. Within the Christian world, the person who tends to write off "Evangelicals" or "Roman Catholics" is not likely to accept a Muslim. This is why the type of group I have described is excellent experience for those training for the ordained ministry. That is so not just for those who will work afterwards in multi-faith areas, though it obviously has special relevance there. It is so for all, because in the course of their ministry they will surely have to cross a number of barriers, and gaining experience of doing so in one context will help them in others. What is sometimes less obvious is that the class barrier is as sharp as cultural or faith barriers. This often stands in the way of any real meeting between a minister coming into an area from the outside and those with whom he will be living and working. In any group or training situation it is easy to see quite quickly who can make this sort of jump across barriers and who cannot.

To make such a jump, what is vital is the quality of imagination or empathy. We may never have been to a Pakistani village, but we can be alongside another so sensitively that we can feel something of what it is like to be there, because that is what is real to the person we are talking to. There are ways that we can convey that empathy, without taking away from the other person the uniqueness of his or her experience. Such imagination requires effort, but means a great deal. We can "feel", if we really listen, what doing Haj (the annual pilgrimage to Mecca) means in our Muslim friend's experience. Perhaps he is telling us that, having been there himself, he is now going for his deceased father who was never able to go. We might begin to understand something of why a Muslim can find the rigorous fasting involved in Ramadan not just a chore and a discipline but a joy and an opportunity.

The opposite of this understanding is shown by a sad story I heard of a Western missionary in Pakistan who deliberately ate his meals in public during Ramadan in order to show his rejection of what he saw as legalism, unnecessary and oppressive. This not only caused offence, but also showed he had no "feel" at all for what this month could mean for a devout Muslim. We may be asked to share natural joy in the unexpected, but can we feel the exhilaration of our friend who tells us about his special blessing from Allah, in that he has been given a permanent job as a fitter in a factory? His Sheikh had told him he had been praying daily for this, and he feels his prayers have been answered. There may be a place for theological discussion about this, but meanwhile we are called to rejoice with him.

The quality here described is essential in anything more than superficial relationship. It is the quality most needed in ministry, and the hardest to teach. It is shown again and again by Jesus who, as St John puts it, knew "what was in a man". It is the quality we instinctively recognize in a person who meets us. Though we have not known him or her for long, perhaps, we feel he or she in some ways knows us better than we know ourselves. It is such persons that we are ready to talk with at a deep level, because we know they stand with us, that they really do listen and understand. It is the quality shown by a woman who visited a place of worship of another faith recently with a group of Christians. They were given a talk by a woman of the other faith. After some time, a man arrived and he simply took over. She politely accepted and deferred to him, but was nearly in tears. In discussion afterwards, it turned out that only the woman among the Christian group had picked this up. She alone knew what had really happened deep down and could "feel" it. She felt that the woman was in some ways caught between cultures and understood her anguish.

How wide are our interests? Do they concern the whole of the life of the person or, at any rate, what the person wishes to reveal? It is easy only to half-listen, as we wait for the discussion really to develop into what we consider worthwhile, for what we have come, the real religious dialogue. If we do this, we are very far from where Jesus was, as he related to the whole of a person's life, and above all to what the other person presented to him as important. Such real listening leads us to identify with secular problems which affect the people we are with, and their community, which may not affect us at all. These include a whole range of areas: education, health, immigration, housing, employment, relations with the police, politics. They may concern the rights of particular faiths — for example, the Muslims' right or otherwise to call people publicly to prayer, using an amplification system. Or their right to slaughter animals in their way, so that the meat is ritually clean. Christians in Britain are seen as people with influence by those of other faiths. Can we show them a solidarity, which may not be particularly in our interests and may require a lot of effort? How do we do this, without trampling on the sensitivity of fellow Christians, who may well think very differently from us? These are not simple questions, but not ones we can easily opt out of in the interests of "pure dialogue". Some are matters of straight justice, matters of equal concern for us all, regardless of our faith. We can work on these more effectively together than apart. Here we can draw on the theological and biblical resources of our faith; these will include the radical social implications of liberation-style theology, which may be something new to friends from another faith. They too may have resources in the area of justice, from their tradition.

One of the British Council guidelines says: "Dialogue makes it possible to share in service to the community." This has not been an easy area for us in our situation. Partly because of the rapid turnover of students every two years, and partly because, though living in the same city, we are not in the same area. This has, in its negativity, taught us the importance of this principle.

We could do so much more if we were living in the same community. Some students are now opting to live in the inner city, and it is hoped that this might lead to more common action. It might also lead to working more directly with local congregations, which are of course the ideal and natural group to be involved in this way.

We have been able in small ways to express our common concern, for South Africa, human rights, etc. One student has recently taken initiatives related to housing conditions, in cooperation with people of other faiths. Much more could and should be done. Because we cannot do everything, and the situation is not ideal, it does not mean we should do nothing and not start at all.

Meeting as persons of faith

We can only begin to meet at this level if sufficient trust has been built up. Hence the importance of all that has been said earlier. The British Council Guidelines make clear that dialogue depends upon mutual understanding and mutual trust. Apart from all that has been said about friendship, it is important here that each group does not suspect in any way the motives of the other group; otherwise there can be no real trust. In our story, neither "side" has felt that one side is using the whole framework, under the cover of "dialogue", to proselytize the other. Some find this hard to understand, and one or two who came casually into the group raised the question, as they cannot see any other motive as compelling or even possible. It is baffling to them when this is vigorously denied by both Christians and Muslims. This suspicion shows what has normally happened when our two religions meet. Great trust is needed from both sides. Many Christians feel that all this is "selling out the gospel", "engaging in syncretism"; from the Muslim perspective, it seems to militate against the stark solidarity of Muslim fundamentalism. From both sides, we need to stand up to such traditional attitudes, and need therefore to have deep trust in each other. Long-term contact with people of other faiths is not a popular or easily understood thing.

To move into the mutual sharing of the understanding of faith is not easy, particularly for those who find it difficult to talk about the deepest things within them. Many Christians naturally avoid discussion or language of the heart, particularly in our European context. If we have had little or no experience of relating to fellow Christians at an articulated faith level, then we are bound to find it hard and very exposing when we meet those for whom such discussion is part of the everyday to-and-fro of life. A Muslim will expect some account from us of where we stand in terms of our faith. By revealing ourselves in this way, we reveal our respect for and trust in him, as he does for us when he speaks of the faith within him. This is often not easy for us, whatever our educational background, since we are not used to talking at this level. We are more used to being talked at in church, rather than talking together. In everyday life, we are used to keeping our faith private, and often in one section of life. We do not articulate it to "outsiders". Practising Muslims usually do not make this separation. Their faith permeates everything they do, and they are not unwilling to acknowledge it. Members of a congregation who wish to engage in real encounter with a group of another faith would do well to have had some experience of really talking to one another. Such sharing has often taken place within more "charismatic, evangelical" churches. The problem here is that this often, but by no means always, goes with an insulated theology which prevents real trust being built up with those of other faiths, in the way we have been discussing.

As we enter the encounter, we are faced inevitably with questions about where our real faith is. These may be expressed directly in questions, or may arise for us in our heart as we listen. We may all have questions and doubts in our faith journey, and that is to be expected. But as we become open in interfaith encounter, such questions as these are likely to arise in our mind. Are we convinced deep down that we are loved and held by God? Do we have a spirituality in which we give space for God really to meet us, and do we really encounter God? Is the Christ we speak of in the discussion merely the Christ of the creeds which we recite on Sundays, or is he truly the Risen Lord who has appeared to us as well as to St Paul, the same Lord who died for us? Far from lacking this personal dimension of the experience of God, as is often thought, I find that the Muslims in our group speak personally of the reality of their relationship with God. If I am convinced too that Christ died for the Muslim brother in front of me, as for me, and convinced deep down, I can then avoid a Christian "superiority", which is so easily there in me if I care to admit it.

Such faith in the Risen Lord can give me a "joy in believing" and a heart overflowing with love, a love not my own but stemming from him. This love it is which will give me a desire to communicate the source from which it comes. It will enable me to transcend my own inarticulateness, not in the sense of using theological terms which are incomprehensible to the listener, but in the direct terms of daily speech. For example what do we do with the eucharist? In our ordinary Christian life we make of it what we will. But in meeting with people of other faiths, how do we explain what it means to us? Do we repeat only dry phrases — or do we really experience it as the gift of God and a sign of the reality of the presence of Christ? If so, how do we put this into words? So too with the scriptures. I may be able to quote this or that verse, and this is not unimportant, as we are with Muslims who know much of their scriptures by heart. But can I show in what way it is the basis for the Good News which I am trying to convey? Overall, do I have a gospel for the Muslim, or for anyone else for that matter? Is that gospel truly liberating and salvific for the whole of life? The Muslim friend will certainly feel he has knowledge of the highest way of life, and will wish to convey that to me.

If encounter is to be real, I am called also to accept the integrity of the faith of my friend. God has revealed himself in many ways, and as a disciple of Christ I follow him because I am convinced that the fullest revelation of God is in him, that he is the way, the truth and the life. This fullest revelation is not just for me, but one that my friends of another faith have the right to know. But nevertheless, I am faced with the question whether they are worshipping the same God as me. Intellectually, I know they must be, as there is only one God, and that is a basic tenet of both our faiths. But deep in my heart, can I feel that they are doing so, even though they do not see God in his complete fullness (if I felt they did, then I would be a Muslim)? If I do not accept this basic question, then there will always be a mental holding back, a distancing. I will always be on the search for the differences between us, and of course this does have a place — but I will not be concerned with what is common and unites us. It was a breakthrough in the ecumenical movement when Christians of different denominations began not only intellectually to comprehend, but also inwardly to feel, how much more there was that united them than divided them. It is facile to suggest that there is little difference between this ecumenism, and the growth in understanding between different faiths. Nevertheless a basis for real encounter is the realization that as we meet with those of other faiths, we are on holy ground together, before the one God.

The British Council Guidelines suggest ways of building up trust. They say: "Christians must avoid misleading and hurtful terminology." I feel that the Muslims in our group have quite clearly done the same. This must apply to occasions when we are together, and also to our normal way of speaking. That makes for greatly increased sensitivity all the time. Two examples. I heard a Christian priest recently speaking to the congregation before the baptism of a baby; he said that we are here to worship "the Christian God", Father, Son and Holy Spirit. I cringed as I thought of all the implications of that in a multifaith context, and the almost tribal limitation of God involved. I think too of the general intercession prayer, in our Church of England communion service (Alternative Service Book). My problems are in the limiting clauses at the end, as we remember "those who have died in the faith of Christ", and commend "ourselves and all Christian people to your unfailing love". Is that love so limited?

We are also asked "not lightly or thoughtlessly to dismiss other religions as human attempts to reach God, with nothing of God's grace in them". Part of trust is accepting as honest statements what our brothers and sisters of another faith say. This is particularly so when those statements are in line with, and not out of joint with what one knows of a person, and his or her way of life. When our Sufi friends talk in terms of grace, and the way God finds them in prayer, and everything they say reveals a close relationship to God, then that is something we must accept as reality. We may interpret this as the power of the Spirit working in their lives, though they do not know it. We may talk of the Logos enlightening everyone who comes into the world. But, in whatever way, God has touched them, and their experience is acknowledged as authentic. So, too, when we feel and experience over a long period love without limit flowing from a devout person of another faith — and I can think of particular examples — we are not entitled to say: I believe that this is just their natural humanity, and has no connection with their faith. They are whole people, and they are what they are because of their faith.

The Guidelines suggest that adherents of other faiths must be allowed to define themselves in their own terms. Much of what we have been doing in our group is exactly this. We may know what we think of Muhammad, but that is interpretation from outside. We should allow the Muslims to interpret Muhammad for us, as we hope they will listen to what we say of St Paul. So also, for example, with the concept of Jihad, which we find unacceptable, with its holy war connotations. But it can be defined spiritually, and quite beautifully, as I have heard. That requires time and patient listening. So also the careful reading of scripture; we have found it helpful to give our interpretation of certain passages of the Qur'an, from the outside; but then we need to hear the exegesis and hermeneutic from within the circle. So in reverse with New Testament passages. And the same will apply to the clarification of social and ethical practices. We may think that we know all about the Muslim way of life in the family. But let us allow them to explain how it fits into the general pattern of their faith.

As we proceed together, a number of things will be happening at the same time. These we will examine in turn. The first is that as Christians we will find ourselves fulfilling what the BCC guidelines call "a responsibility to clear away misconceptions in others about what we believe and teach". The well-known example here is of course the Trinity, and the question of whether we worship three gods. It has been a great challenge for our students to have to state, with careful thought, what this might mean to those who are not within our own hermeneutical circle, and do not have our faith experience. They have to address the question first to themselves as to whether this is really important to them, or just an inherited dogma, not really able to be talked about because not really experienced. Alternatively, it may be a real experience but so hard to put adequately into words. But we have no other instrument if we are to communicate it at all. The same with the meaning of the cross. I was in the house of a Muslim during Holy Week this year, with a ministerial student. There was a West Indian convert to Islam there, too. He told us of a disturbing dream he had had about heaven, in which his Christian grandmother featured prominently. He asked me to interpret the dream. I suggested it might have to do with guilt about giving up the Christian faith, and his subconscious worry about meeting his grandmother in the afterlife. He replied that he did not consciously feel such guilt, because he was sure he had found the true faith. He asked me how I, who had travelled in many parts of the world, found it difficult to agree with him. I replied that it had something to do with what I felt was revealed about the nature of God and God's relationship with us, as seen in the events of Holy Week, Good Friday and Easter. As a well-tutored new Muslim, he said: "What can Good Friday mean, because God could not let a chosen prophet suffer and die? And no such could possibly cry 'My God, my God, why have you forsaken me?'"

I asked my student to respond. He began to go into the differences between the Gospels, and whether Jesus actually said those words or not. There is clearly a place for such a discussion, but I felt that what was being sought was something definite, and what was being heard, valid as it might be for a discussion among Christians, was only adding confusion. I moved the discussion on to what I felt were the misconceptions involved. We do not accept that there are things that God "cannot do". Nor is the Christ on the cross a special prophet, but in a real sense God himself. The cry is important as part of his essential identity with us as human beings. His going through death is crucial for us. A Muslim, of course, cannot agree with this, but he or she has a right to know where we stand.

Nor do we need to duck the real differences in attitudes to certain ethical and social questions. We need to explain that it is not because of "permissiveness" and slackness that we have a different view, but that it may stem from the preconceptions of our faith. When I visited Pakistan, I had a number of talks with Muslims. They were of course fascinated by the fact that my sister had married a Pakistani Muslim, and indeed become a Muslim. They invariably asked what the attitude of my family was. I replied that, though it was not easy for them at first — my father is an Anglican priest — they had supported her through it all, and indeed welcomed my brother-in-law into the family. They found this very hard to understand. Did my father not punish her? Did he not cast her out? I explained that he did not, and this reflects, among other things, an experience of God as love, and love without limit, as shown in Jesus Christ, in his teaching, his parables and his life itself. Most were uncomprehending, but one notable exception was a university lecturer. He thought hard and said: "Yes, perhaps you have something to teach us there."

It is important that we also are prepared to admit it when Islam may have something to teach us. Clear examples might be in the area of prayer and fasting, and also in giving to the community. May we not learn something too from the grace of personality of those we meet? We may ourselves be challenged to look again at our spirituality, our theology, and our strength of commitment to those around us. We can find ourselves with a new depth of commitment to Christ, a new understanding of his decisive revelation of the nature of God, at the same time as setting this beside a new clarification of the beliefs of others. We may at times be put to shame as we reflect on the half-heartedness of much of what we do, with all our wealth and historical influence. We may find, as I have been privileged to find in a man like Zaheer, someone who shows qualities of love, gentleness, pastoral insight and spirituality that sometimes fill me with wonder. He has, if anyone has, the qualities described by St Paul, as the fruits of the Spirit — love, joy, peace, patience, kindness, goodness, fidelity, gentleness and self-control. Are they any less the fruits of the Spirit because he is not aware that they are?

In the encounter we will be challenged to self-criticism as we look at our own faith and the practice of it. Yet often we try vainly to defend the indefensible. Here surely we are being defensive of ourselves, and not of Christ, however much we try to fool ourselves. If he is the Lord we say he is, we surely do not need to be over-protective of him. We can accept the horror stories of church history, and indeed of the contemporary Christian world as we are faced with questions about the reality of the Crusades, or of Northern Ireland today. We need to face the questioning of the so-called Christian ethos and values of Western society, where competition and the pursuit of individual gain are tending to become ultimate values; where the family is exalted but is breaking up on all sides because of the pressures it is under. Here so often the only ethical guide left is individual whim. We may also have to face hard questions about the scriptures where lie the roots of our faith. We may have to face the possibility of accepting, when talking with a Jewish person, that the roots of antisemitism can perhaps be traced to the New Testament. We are not required to defend every instruction of St Paul, such that it can be read off and applied in our different contexts today. Our attitude to scripture is different from that of a Muslim. So, women do not have to wear hats in church today, and we can be happy about it and not defensive. Discussion around such things can help the Muslim see how we do exegesis, and how we apply passages, and we need not be apologetic about it. Rather, it can help him to see that we feel liberated by what we see as constructive, and not destructive, in our approach to the New Testament.

The counterpoint to this self-criticism is that there may be times for what, in counselling terms, would be called "caring confrontation" with someone of another faith. In a counselling relationship, or one of friendship, this would not advisedly happen until real empathy had been established. But if this has happened, then we may feel we should "speak the truth in love" (Eph. 4:15), when occasion demands. There is a point when any relationship must face this test, and it will be all the easier if we have been self-critical ourselves. There may, for example, come a point when we wish to say firmly and clearly that we are not prepared to hear, say, any more about the Gospel of Barnabas (a later work often being quoted by Muslims as being nearer to the truth than our four Gospels, and which denies the crucifixion). Rather than complaining about this to ourselves after the meeting, let us say it clearly, within the trust of the relationship. We have to say that we consider that a much later work and unreliable, and that there is no point in proceeding with our discussion unless they are prepared to talk about the canonical Gospels. We are prepared to discuss on the basis of the scriptures the Muslim presents to us — the Qur'an and the Hadith — and so if we are to proceed, it must be on the basis of the scriptures we put forward. And as we lament our own divisions, we may wish to contradict suggestions that there is a united Islamic brotherhood, as we look at the tragic divisions of the modern Muslim world. When we hear about Allah as the compassionate and the merciful one, we may wish to question when the claim is made by hijackers and terrorists who have no hesitation in shedding innocent blood. When we are told of the tolerance of Islam, then the treatment of the Bahais or Anglicans in Iran may also have to be put on the agenda for discussion from our side. It can be a sign of the strength of the relationship if such questions are then taken up constructively, and can lead us together to accept our failures to live up to either of our faiths, and together to call upon the God who forgives.

Sometimes we can be over-cautious. I remember taking a parish group to a large and rather bare mosque. I had prepared them carefully, asking them to listen and not argue back, remembering that they were guests. Also that the women should wear long skirts to cover their legs out of respect for Muslim custom. We heard from the Imam about how Muslims respect Jesus as a great prophet. One of the women in our group interrupted and said quite simply: "Yes, but he is much more than that." Again, the Imam explained that they have no music in the mosque, and gave his reasons. The same woman intervened and said: "How gloomy and flat that must make things!" Far from leading to problems, this led to a most helpful discussion of the basis of our belief and the nature of worship. My instruction about clothing had been disregarded by one of the women. The prayers had actually begun, when a Pakistani Muslim came over and politely put a blanket over her legs as she sat. She turned to me and said, rather loudly, that she would not have a filthy Pakistani blanket over her legs. I suggested that she should leave the prayer hall, if she would not cover her legs. As we talked, a young black Muslim came up and took her by the arm, and invited her to go with him upstairs to the gallery. What discussion they had there I do not know, but when the prayer came to an end, she came down looking calm, and said: "What a charming young man!" A good example of pastoral care?

Finally, in the area of faith, we come to the place of witness. The British Council Guidelines suggest that dialogue becomes the means of authentic witness. Debate has taken place as to whether the article "the" is appropriate here, or whether we should substitute "a". Many are apprehensive about the very word "dialogue", as they see it as an opting out of "evangelism" and as a substitute for the primary calling of Christians to tell the Good News. But our experience is that it is nothing of the kind. Again and again we are called to give witness through meeting in dialogue. That is why it is so exposing for ordinary Christians. Experience shows that we give witness normally here or not at all. Those who suspect the idea of dialogue very often end up by not giving any witness at all to people of other faiths. For the witness stems from the meeting, which is the essence of dialogue. In a long-term relationship like the one I have described, such a witness comes naturally and by request. It is in no way imposed, but expected by the partner. And so, though we recognize there may be other ways of authentic witness — large open meetings, street-to-street visiting, direct invitations to church, etc. — in practice we wonder whether these often happen, and when they do, whether the witness has much chance of really being "heard". And so the "a" in theory, often becomes "the" in practice.

At one of our meetings, a visiting Muslim began to hand out Islamic tracts for us to read, stating clearly the superiority of Islam. Some of our students objected to this. I said that this was what in practice Christian missionaries have been doing over the years, and in the right situation it has been one of the means of spreading the gospel. But how effective it is in our situation is shown perhaps by the negative response we felt. This is not to say that from time to time people's lives have not been changed by reading a tract. We are not to prescribe for God. But as a norm, in our situation, it is through personal meeting that we find the means of authentic witness. And, in reverse, of course, we must expect to hear the authentic witness of persons of other faiths.

None of this is to say that dialogue is simply a covert means of proselytization. What happens in the meeting is in God's hands and not ours. We shall come back to this point later.

Meeting as persons of prayer

Our story, which began as one of quest for dialogue, friendship and understanding, has developed also into an experience of shared spirituality. It is here that some of the more controversial questions may be raised.

When we have prayed together, it was based upon a shared commitment to the quest for mutual understanding in which we have all been involved. It did not happen on one-off occasions, or early on, but only when we had come to know each other sufficiently, to trust each other's integrity and to have a great deal of mutual respect. This respect is not only for each other as persons, but also as persons of faith, whose life and being are somehow held by God, and acknowledged to be so, and who are sincerely attempting to work out the implications in their daily lives. There is a congruity between faith and life. There has also been sufficient common ground for each group to affirm that all are worshipping the one God, and that God, though seen differently in certain respects, is recognizably the same in nature (of course, there are differences in the way individual Christians see God, and they still pray together). Seeing God in Christ does of course make a great difference, and could make it impossible to pray together with those whose view of God is contradictory to that shown in Christ. But that has not been our experience. And so the form of prayer that is used by both has been similar in content and in the understanding of the relationship between God and the believer. With the particular group of Muslims we have been fortunate to be with, there is also a common sense of grace, and the understanding that we are nothing before the greatness of God, totally dependent on God's mercy, and always in need of God's forgiveness. Kenneth Cracknell, in his book *Towards a New Relationship*,[1] refers to an episode re-corded in 2 Kings 10. Jehu asks Jehonadab: "Is your heart true to my heart as mine is to yours?" Jehonadab answers: "It is," and Jehu says: "If it is, give me your hand." John Wesley, in his sermon 34, uses this as a text to introduce the question of shared spirituality. He is of course talking about Christians, but in our interfaith context, we feel we have been able to answer Yes, with Jehonadab, and it is on the basis of this "heart relationship" that we can pray together. At one of our meetings, a German Lutheran theological professor was present. It was the first time he had been to England, and he sat through the meeting, shared the food, and listened to the prayers from both sides. He remarked afterwards that if anyone had told him beforehand that he would be able to say "Yes" to everything that a Muslim had prayed, and add his Amen, he would have laughed at him. But such had been the atmosphere he had encountered that he felt himself carried through into ready assent. He could have said that he had been led by the Spirit, as indeed we feel we have been.

Such joint prayer began with a clear request from a Muslim. It did not begin with our agonizing over whether we should have prayer at our meetings, and under what conditions. It happened naturally. It was based upon a felt need, and a recognition by Zaheer that my prayers were real and something he desired for his daughter. It was my sensitivity to him, not the limitations that he imposed, that determined the actual form of words used. The whole thing was at a personal level where there was a mutual sense of "meeting in the cave of the heart". We have not kept silence together, but I am sure that we could; and such a silence would be in the presence of God.

The shared prayer was based too on real need, and on shared public concern. Handsworth, Soweto, human rights, are all situations where Christians and Muslims are equally concerned, with which we can equally identify. There may be other situations where it is possible to engage in common action and where prayer can stem naturally from that, as each faith provides from its own tradition resources for movement forward. These will be areas where theological differences will not be primary, but what unites us are the ethical implications of our faiths. This has been felt as we have prayed around areas of the world where Christians and Muslims have been tragically divided, such as Lebanon. Or where Christian and Christian, or Muslim and Muslim have been killing members of their own faith, in the name of the same God. But as well as these wider concerns, we have not been afraid to offer prayer for the daily needs of our two communities, in common citizenship in the same place. So also for family needs at a particular time. Such is the stuff of daily prayer for each of us, and it has been good to share it together in common humanity.

When prayer leaves the private or semi-private area, between two people or within a closed group, it becomes a different situation. In the prayer in a public place of worship, as in St Martin's Church, anyone may come to the prayer, and indeed it is hoped that those who are not part of the group will do so. It then becomes very important to recognize that people come with all sorts of assumptions and experiences. It is crucial, therefore, that no one feels imposed upon, or carried to where they do not wish to be. It is right to specify that people should feel free to pray in each other's company, one keeping reverent silence while the other prays. They should feel no pressure to join in, even silently. The Methodist Church Working Party on Multi-Faith Society talks of communal acts of successive declarations of faith, where "each community was intending and was recognized by other communities to be intending to honour God... We might say that while one community was exhibiting their devotion, the others were only required to be spectators, however sympathetic. Individuals were allowed the inner freedom to go further, if their conscience permitted." The Roman Catholic Church states in *Guidelines for a Dialogue between Muslims and Christians*:[2] "Some people ask if we can pray with Muslims. Although it is evident that we cannot take part actively in the cult of another religion, we can be associated with spontaneous prayer." The prayer we have been talking about is such prayer. It is also rather less "staged" than some specific interfaith services. These may be annual occasions, or arranged around such general themes as "peace". Nevertheless, there have been good examples of these in our area; for example, the annual worship of the interfaith group in Wolverhampton.

But in general, it is important that everyone can be where they wish to be, in relation to what is before them. Or rather, we would hope, where they will allow the Holy Spirit to take them, as they are open to be led by what is put before them. It may be that they are led simply to recognize a genuine spirituality in those of another faith, though they cannot share it. That will itself be a great step forward, at a time when many are led by normal ignorance or prejudice.

There is a clear difference between attending the worship of another faith, with a sense of respect and for gaining understanding, on the one hand, and sharing in prayer on the other. In particular, with Islam and Christianity, there is a difference between the regular, prescribed five-times daily prayer and praying together informally. To stand shoulder to shoulder with Muslims at that point, and to go through the actions to the accompaniment of the words of the prayer leader, is to acknowledge that we are part of that faith community, which we are not.

This is not to say we cannot have profound respect for such obeisance before God, or for the way it symbolizes solidarity between believers, as seen in so many different parts of the world and in such different circumstances. One inevitably thinks of the Christian eucharist. It is one of the two central sacraments of the Christian faith, and a "celebration of the Lord's death until he comes". As such, we hope it preaches a message to those of another faith who might be present, of a unity in Christ across all barriers of race, culture and sex. It is also, though this is difficult for a Muslim to understand, a proclamation of the centrality of the cross and of the presence of Christ. We would hope too that being present at the eucharist may add to his or her understanding of what Christian worship is about; participation, however, would not be appropriate, or wished for, particularly in the case of a Muslim. It may well be different for a Sikh or a Hindu. For them, the eucharist seems superficially like the sharing of "prasadam" (blessed food). And this is offered to everyone who comes to a temple. To take it involves no faith commitment, and many Christians will receive it willingly. The meaning of the eucharist needs to be explained simply and clearly to whoever is coming, as well as its link with full Christian commitment. To be left out may hurt the visitor a little, but that is necessary if we are to be true to the integrity of our faith, and my experience is that our reasons will be accepted.

This is partly the result of the difference between an all-inclusive faith such as Hinduism, and one which is credal, like Christianity and Islam, and which is therefore at times exclusive. It is partly that the eucharist is connected with baptism, which is a sign of membership as well as a sacrament of incorporation into the Lord's death and resurrection. To explain these things can be a positive way into useful dialogue. Hindus may find it difficult to see why a Christian cannot participate in all the rituals of their faith when, say, attending a Hindu temple. From their point of view, there is no bar on our joining in full veneration of the image, receiving of the sacred fire and ash, etc. Some Christians have done this, justifying it theologically. Here, St Paul's injunction about considering the conscience of the weaker brethren (1 Cor. 10) may be relevant. Paul was talking of taking food offered to idols, not about actually venerating them. This "food" is the equivalent of the prasadam, and eating it is one level of participation. Going further is another question. It may be that there is a difference here from prayers at home, when one is with friends, where it comes more into the type of context described in the diary. It may make a difference, too, who one is. If one is a representative minister, and recognizable as such, then one is inevitably seen as acting for the whole church. And can one so commit the whole church? But a layman or woman may feel freer.

Witnessing worship in a Hindu temple is a complex experience for a Christian with little background of Hindu practices. There is the initial barrier of seeing all the gods, in seemingly garish colours, and reacting from one's own theological position. Can one think of them as "images" rather than as "idols"? And even then, are they "graven images"? Male and female? Roger Hooker's book, *What is Idolatry?*[3] may be a help at this point. The worship too is so far from our normal experience, in a different language, with loud instruments, and the blowing of the conch shell. People appear to be going here and there as it goes on, with little sense of order, and children seem to be free to do what they will.

My experience is that people react to all these in very different ways. It is often those who find the temple difficult who are impressed by the mosque; and with others it is completely the other way. What we bring to each is our own personal agenda, which includes what we like in Christian worship. If we are for austerity and discipline and quiet and unity, then we will tend to appreciate the mosque. If we are for joy and colour and music, and are not particularly for order as we understand it, we will tend to prefer the temple. If we are bothered by noise and disruption by children in a Christian service, we will prefer the mosque; if we resent that children cannot feel at home in church, then we will be excited by the way children can come and go as they please in the temple. If we feel strongly about women's participation, we will enjoy the leading part women have in the temple, and the way families are there all together. The absence of women in the mosque may well put us off. We bring too our own theological agenda; if we like a strong and dogmatic faith, and one easily defined, then we will prefer Islam. If we are much more awakened by a sense of search, with an open-ended theology, then we will find Hinduism easier, as we feel included in a common journey.

Different again may be a visit to a Buddhist Vihara. Here the main activity may be meditation. Full participation is much easier, as we are free in our mind to meditate on Christ, or a biblical phrase, or say the Jesus prayer, or reflect on a common idea like compassion, which would unite us with the Buddhists around. One of our students who undertook a long-term placement in a Theravada Centre says: "To learn about Buddhism really means to meditate with Buddhists. The doctrines and the theory can be read about, but Buddhism is centred upon the practice of meditation, and the fellowship and the dialogue consist of sharing this experience. It is in the spontaneity of this experience that we begin to realize what is indeed written on our hearts and what is given us to pray. This deepens my faith. In seeking to put this into words, we are faced with conflicting beliefs, but the sense of sharing remains."

Having said this, it is good, I believe, to bring people of other faiths to witness Christian worship, including the eucharist. For, at its best, it is a proclamation of the good news. In the Indian prison where I was chaplain, we eventually opened up the eucharist to Hindus who wished to come forward and receive the elements, explaining clearly the full meaning on each occasion. These were prisoners who could not be baptized because of their circumstances, and whom anyway it would not be good to baptize away from their families. As life prisoners, many of them had been part of the congregation for years. They came because they saw proclaimed there the forgiveness of God in Christ. How then to exclude them at the eucharist, which is *the* moment of the declaration of forgiveness? We did for some time, but it never felt right, particularly as some of the Christians present were very nominally so. We changed eventually after considerable debate; one of the reasons was the words of a particular prisoner, who had killed his elder brother, and could not feel forgiven. We explained that the words of the service were directed at him as at any other full participant. Yes, he understood this, but he could not feel it, unless he could kneel shoulder to shoulder with us, and receive the body and blood of Christ. As Moltmann has put it in his book *The Open Church*,[4] what needs to be justified at the eucharist is the exclusion, but we have decided that what needs to be justified is inclusion. All that I am saying is that there may be occasions to include someone of another faith in the eucharist. But what we have been talking about here are not such occasions.

We come next to the vexed question of what words we are to use in praying together. With silence there is no difficulty, but if we are to go beyond that, how inclusive should our language be? As can be seen from the diary, our own way has been to be as inclusive as possible, within our own integrity. Prayer is addressed to God. An assumption we work with is that when the Christian speaks of God, and the Muslim of Allah, we are speaking of the same God. I personally do not pray on such occasions with the words "through Jesus Christ our Lord". For Jesus is not the Lord acknowledged by half the people present. And so I usually use the words "in thy name". Those present can interpret as they wish, and for me it is in the name of Jesus. For others it is in the name of God, or Allah. Again, I would not use a Trinitarian blessing, but the Aaronic one from the Old Testament, which I use much anyway: "Unto God's gracious mercy and protection we commit you. The Lord bless you and keep you. The Lord make his face to shine upon you and be gracious unto you. The Lord lift his countenance upon you, and give you his peace."

In terms of the content of the prayer, I would follow what I would normally do in any extempore prayer. I would pray according to the needs of the situation, and what is right for the people in front of me, very much guided by the Spirit — who, as St Paul says, supplies the words when we do not know how to pray — even if the Spirit is not specifically named. My prayer, I hope, would be filled with the love of Christ. His death and resurrection would not be absent from the occasion, as I am very conscious that he died and rose for these friends in front of me, just as much as for myself. I am conscious, as Roger Hooker has put it, that "we have submitted ourselves to the patient and humble discipline of listening to others (those before me), of being content to spend time with them, *because God loves them infinitely more than we do*."[5] This surely moves me to pray in a way that is inclusive of them.

I do not believe this is a "cop-out", as some may feel. Prayer is not the time for proselytization, but for meeting before God and receiving from God. It is not a time for expressing doctrinal statements and pinning people to them, but for laying ourselves open before God. If it is the Spirit in whom we meet, then even outwardly exclusive words may do no harm, for integrity and empathy mark the situation. If it is not, no amount of carefully chosen words can make an inclusive prayer.

We have used psalms from the Old Testament, and these can be very effective. They can help a sensitive Muslim to see the beauty in some Jewish scripture which, in the tragic divide between Jew and Muslim, can only be a good thing. Psalms and prayers about creation, the law of the Lord, suffering, patience, forgiveness, humility — all these can strike common human chords. So also passages about being uplifted by the hand of God, and God's infinite love for us.

On the Muslim side, I have again been impressed by how, within the limits possible, they have tried to "include". They begin, as they are obliged to, by reciting a passage from the Qur'an in Arabic; they will then usually translate it. And as mentioned in the diary, when Muhammad is spoken of, they will usually follow this with a mention of the prophet Jesus. We have been relating mainly to those influenced by the Sufi tradition. But those who are not, and who have prayed with us, have also shown the same concern. We know there are more exclusive sentiments in the Qur'an than are being used when we meet. But, of course, the same can be said of our scriptures. We are looking for what unites us, not controversial issues that divide.

Prayer with a Hindu is a rather different matter. Since he or she does not have an exclusive approach, we can pray more or less freely. There is no problem about Jesus as Lord, though I would surely not wish to pray at this point about "Jesus as the one and only Lord". When I am asked to pray for healing I would pray clearly in the name of Jesus; the Hindu has seen Jesus as a power for healing, and that is why he wants me to pray. I might well do the same with a Muslim if he is asking me to pray as a Christian minister.

In all this, as Kenneth Cracknell has pointed out in his book,[6] the best Christian prayer is the Lord's Prayer. It is a prayer that, apart perhaps from the first phrase "Our Father" which a Muslim cannot use of God, is widely embracing of people of other faiths. For it is a prayer about human longing, about the coming of the kingdom of God, about bread eschatological and daily, about the need for God's forgiveness and to forgive one another. As such, it is a prayer we should be prepared to share with others, and not just reserve as our property as baptized Christians. There may also be texts which Muslims use that we can accept for ourselves as they are. These often come from the Sufi tradition. They can be seen in such books as *The Oxford Book of Prayer*,[7] *The One who Listens*,[8] and the study of Muslim prayer manuals by Constance Padwick.[9]

We could go beyond all these in the search of a common spirituality in the more mystical sense. Glimpses of this can be seen in the common longing for God and growth in the spiritual life, going alongside a discipline of life, which characterizes the Sufi orders, and such orders as the Franciscans. It can be seen in certain common elements in Sufism and some aspects of the modern charismatic movement. Are there ways that the Spirit, rather than being a symbol of division as part of the Trinity, can still be seen as God moving within us in prayer in the depths of our being? Romans 8:26ff talks of how, when we do not know how to pray, it is the Spirit within us that makes articulate our struggling and groaning. Even in the Qur'an, Allah is presented as being closer to us than our jugular vein.

Common too is the idea of growth in the life of prayer, which is a gift of God. What we need to do is to make ourselves available to receive that gift, giving space to God. It comes most easily for many of us when there is a balance between what Bonhoeffer calls "prayer and righteous action". This is what we seem to see in the lives of these particular Muslims, and what perhaps they respond to in those they meet.

When all this has been said and accepted, nevertheless there will always be an element of risk, and at times of doubt. Have we gone too far? Are we being loyal to our Lord Jesus Christ? Is there some unknown side to the Muslims we are meeting which is going to exploit what we are doing? Do they really accept us? Do they really worship the One whom they speak of, and who seems the same God as the One we worship?

When we seem, like this, to have stepped over the abyss and want to jump back, we need then most to affirm our commitment to Christ. It is with him that we are going forward. It was the disciples who were afraid when he went on the way, leading them to Jerusalem. Kenneth Cracknell writes about "this ability to be in uncertainties, mysteries, doubts, without an irritable reaching after fact and reason, alongside a controlling vision of Jesus, and commitment to him". [10] It is a sign, I hope, not of our lack of commitment to Christ, but of our trust in him and his guidance (however faltering as disciples we may be) that we have been able to go at least as far as we have in what the British Council Guidelines calls "a fellow pilgrimage with others who are seeking a new future".

Theological reflection on meeting

In all this, what sort of theology of interfaith dialogue do we find ourselves affirming? *Exclusive, pluralist* and *inclusive* seem to have become the "trinity" of words to describe the positions which can be taken. [11] They have become almost "traditional" and overworked terms. They are clearly useful as a framework, and that is why they have stuck. The problem, I feel — and others have felt — is to remain in one such neat slot all the time. It is important too, I believe, to allow one's theology in this area to be formed and influenced by actual experience of the reality of encounter with people of other faiths, and not to enter into that encounter with a theology all worked out. If that is the way you begin, then you will just find what you want to find.

What follows is quite inadequate, but it is all that space permits, and in any case so much has been written about it. I merely attempt to indicate the kind of theology which, for me, has emerged out of our particular experience. It has been good, too, to see how the theology of others has also been formed by reflection around these experiences.

A fully exclusivist position as regards other faiths would seem to suggest that whatever apparently good things we have experienced with our Muslim friends was purely on the human level. In terms of ultimate salvation, unless they come to acknowledge Christ in the full sense as Saviour, then they cannot be part of God's kingdom. Whatever revelation or experience they have of God is only a beginning at most; only through Christ and the scriptures which witness to him can they find true revelation in its finality. Accepting him means accepting him in incarnation, the cross and the resurrection, as the Son of God. It means being incorporated into him through baptism and membership in his church. And on this does salvation depend. Our friends have not done this, and so, good people as they are, they cannot be saved. This is an over-simplification, but gives an indication of the position. Islam usually takes the same position in reverse, that it is the ultimate revelation and the only way forward; but it often allows for other people of the Book, Christians and Jews, to be included, though not always.

I would not wish to hold to such a position as a whole, though I do hold strongly to the positives within that — to who Christ is, and to what he has done in an ultimate sense. I cannot account for the goodness I have seen in my friends as purely a human phenomenon; it is something that stems from faith, and I cannot see them as being outside the love of God revealed in the very same Christ. This applies too to my friends of faiths other than Islam, and indeed to my sister and brother-in-law.

I would, however, wish to use the word "exclude" in a more limited sense. I would wish to be exclusive of certain things within all faiths. These would be things like casteism within Hinduism, for example, and certain forms of very prevalant village Hinduism, rarely described in books, involving crude animal sacrifices and wild forms of ecstatic behaviour; within Islam Jihad as physical holy war; ultimate non-theism in Buddhism; the denial of Jesus as the Messiah in Judaism. They would include too certain historical manifestations of Christianity, such as the attitude towards Jews through most of our history, the theological position of the Dutch Reformed Church in South Africa as it has linked itself with apartheid, or the triumphalist anti-communism of certain types of Christianity in the United States. We can each make our own list and it is seemingly and sadly endless. Such exclusion is on the basis of our understanding of God as revealed in Jesus Christ and what that has to say of our view of the world. It is based too on his proclamation of the kingdom of God and the character of that kingdom, and Jesus' teaching in the Sermon on the Mount and in the parables. It is based above all on the experience of his life, death and resurrection. Such a view would exclude any theology, within whatever faith, which suggests the world is not real, or that the flesh is inherently bad, or that good will not ultimately triumph over evil, or a theology that would deny that the poor and oppressed are not in some sense God's special concern, and that justice, peace and reconciliation are not central values, or that God is not a God of mercy, justice and, above all, love. I arrive at this through my affirmation of Jesus Christ; his ministry and his teaching provide the criteria for such judgment. I cannot, therefore, merely go along with what our friends may say of the honoured place they give to Jesus.

The *pluralist* view has the advantage of removing the scandal and difficulty in relating to people of other faiths. We can each be content with where we are, for we are each on the path to God that is natural to us. It has the advantage that we can each learn from each other without rivalry, for example, about prayer and meditation, or worship, or caring for our neighbour. We can each be inspired by the great men and women of all our faiths. There are many areas where I believe we can be genuinely pluralist. There are many examples of this in the story we have told.

But if we are to be true to our respective faiths, to our experience of God, and to a truth which we feel is in some sense objective reality and not just subjective to each community, then there are areas which we are bound to find incompatible. We have often found this in our journey together. The cross is a scandal, and always has been. Jesus cannot be the Christ of St John's Gospel, and of Colossians and Romans and Hebrews, and not in some way cause offence. The New Testament witness is not about a good and loving man who gave his life for his vision of the kingdom of God and so became an inspiration to all men and women at all times, including ourselves. To accept Jesus on such terms would remove many difficulties. He would be like the Buddha or Gandhi or, for that matter, St Francis. But it does not do justice to the New Testament record, or any significant part of it. And, as Christians, if we do not start there, I do not know where we can start. Nor do I think that such a position in the end helps dialogue. We need to help others encounter the real Christian witness, not something adjusted to make things easier.

Moreover, there are certain incompatibilities which the pluralist case does not seem to take sufficiently into account. Our eschatological hope is either in the resurrection to some form of eternal life with God, or it is in reincarnation to a higher life on this earth. It is hard to see how we can hold both at the same time, or that the difference is trivial. For many Hindus salvation is absorption into God. It is ultimate non-being in Buddhism. In Christianity and Islam it is to be in a relationship of joy and bliss with God, and with those whom we love. It cannot be all at the same time. We can either hold to the ethic of "an eye for an eye and a tooth for a tooth", or that of turning the other cheek and not returning evil for evil, but overcoming evil with good. Converts from one faith to another are those who witness in a special way that it matters a great deal to which faith they belong. They often face great difficulties, and they may be cast out from their own communities. But they rarely slip back, as they are clear about the distinctiveness of the faith which they have accepted. This has been my experience with the converts I have known in South India. I have rejoiced with them in their baptism, as they experienced it as new life, and been alongside them as they have often faced predictable difficulties. No one would die for the pluralist position, attractive as it is for building up relationships between people of different faiths. Moreover, if each faith is to be an equal spoke of the wheel with God at the centre, as the favourite image has it, then can anything serve as a spoke? If not, how do we decide? As a Christian, my criteria for decision come from my faith, not just because it is mine, but because I believe it gives the nearest we can get to truth.

If forced, then, to come down in one position, I would be an *inclusivist*. I do believe that the meetings I have described are in the presence of the one God. I would follow then a "Logos Christology". It is that the Jesus of Nazareth who is at the centre of the Christian faith is also the Word, working in the creation of all human beings, and that it is in his spirit that they respond to him. John Taylor[12] writes: "The eternal Spirit has been at work in all ages and in all cultures making men aware and evoking their response, and always the one to whom he was pointing and bearing witness was the Logos, the Lamb slain before the foundation of the world." As I meet people of deep integrity in other faiths, such as Zaheer and Qazi and others, I know I must include them in some way. It is through the Logos, which lightens all who come into the world, or through an understanding of the Spirit, that I can best do this. I must include them too within the salvation which God offers, and intends for us. If I can love them, surely God loves them infinitely more. If I wish to include them surely God does too, and much more than I do. God's means of showing this is the cross and resurrection of Jesus Christ. In him God enters fully into our world, identified fully with all men and women, and in going through death to new life, Christ became first fruits of a new creation. Jesus Christ breaks down the barrier between Jew and Gentile, and between humanity and God. He is the liberator of the poor and alienated, those specifically blessed in the Beatitudes. It is through our experience of the cross and the resurrection that we affirm the inclusiveness of the event for all.

Important too is the revelation in the Old Testament of the universal Creator God, that we are all children of the same heavenly Father, whether Jew or Gentile, Christian, Muslim or Hindu. The early covenants are with all humanity, through Adam and Eve and Noah. God will not ultimately abandon creation. This is the witness of the Jewish people, chosen for this task, and at their best when fulfilling the covenant with Abraham, to bring blessing to all people.

There are various forms of inclusive theology within the Roman Catholic and Protestant churches, and many of these stem from deep personal involvement with people of other faiths. I think of such writers as John Taylor and Roger Hooker, or a Roman Catholic like Klostermaier. As I was completing this, I found very helpful, too, an article by Bishop Anasthasios, "Emerging Perspectives of the Relationships of Christians to People of Other Faiths: an Eastern Orthodox Contribution".[13] Projected here is an inclusive theology of other faiths, based in the Logos, the Creator God, and the Spirit. The paper shows how such thinking is not new within the Orthodox tradition. And it gives most interesting historical examples of dialogue between Christians and Muslims within the Byzantine Empire. We so often feel we in the West have suddenly discovered this area of mission, and find it so hard to look historically into the past and geographically into the areas of the world where the church has always lived with other faiths.

It is in our confidence in Christ, then, that we do not feel afraid of being inclusive, as we approach those of other faiths.

We are following the advice in the Epistle to the Philippians (4:8): "Finally, brethren, whatever is true, whatever is honourable, whatever is just, whatever is pure, whatever is lovely, whatever is gracious, if there is any excellence, if there is anything worthy of praise, think about these things." We have seen such things, as have all those who have moved closely with those of other faiths.

The simplicity of life of a South Indian Hindu woman who has the sense of detachment that enables her to give a clear message to those around her: "Whether I live or die, I am the Lord's." Within that ultimate security, she gives out so much love to others. The row upon row of Muslim men, prostrate in prayer, each morning and evening in so many mosques in the midst of a Westernized, secular city. The witness of a young Western Buddhist about to go on a four-year retreat as a novice monk, and who testifies to how he has been saved from a hopeless life of drug addiction through this new faith. The witness of peace of Buddhists, as they walk in procession in nearly every demonstration for nuclear disarmament here in Britain. The unshakeable faith in God displayed by the Jewish community, even in the deepest darkness of the Warsaw Ghetto, as they recited the psalms daily, and sang a song they had learnt from the Vilna Ghetto:

> Never say that you have reached the very end,
> though leaden skies a bitter future may portend,
> and the hour for which we've yearned will yet arrive,
> and our marching step will thunder, "We'll survive."
> From green palm trees to the land of the bitter snow,
> we are here with our sorrow, our woe,
> and whenever our blood was shed in pain,
> our fighting spirits will now resurrect again.

In all this, it is the well-known words of Max Warren that often come to mind:[14]

> Our first task in approaching another people, another culture, is to take off our shoes, for the place we are approaching is holy. Else we may find ourselves treading on men's dreams. More serious still, we may forget that God was here before our arrival. We have then to ask what is the authentic religious content in the experience of the Muslim, the Hindu, the Buddhist, or whoever he may be. We may, if we have asked humbly and respectfully, still reach the

conclusion that our brothers have started from a false premise and reached faulty conclusions. But we must not arrive at our judgment from outside their religious tradition. We have to try to sit where they sit, to enter sympathetically into the pains and griefs and joys of their history, and see how those pains and griefs and joys have determined the premises of their argument. We have, in a word, to be "present" with them.

In that "being present", there may well be pain too. John Taylor[15] records a meeting with a missionary in North India who had introduced him to the reading of a classic of Hindu devotion. He exclaimed, after hearing the way these poems expressed love for the ever-present God: "Surely the missionary task is simply to name him who has for so long been loved, but nameless." But his friend answered: "It's not as simple as that. The agony of this fellowship with the Hindu brother is that the very moment when he and I seem to be saying the same thing in closest unity of experience, I am most aware of the absolute gulf that separates us." This is always real, even in our closest encounters. There is always that gulf, about how we acknowledge Jesus. He is the one we most deeply want to share, and that is because he is the deepest part of our experience. We long for Zaheer and Iqbal and Nazir and Qazi to see him as we see him. We long for that too, I suppose, with our own nominal Christian brothers and sisters, sons and daughters, who see him just as a good example; they would like to follow him, but cannot. It would be easier to follow one of the trends today, and to emphasize God rather than Jesus, in the interests of smooth interfaith relationships. But we cannot escape the call of St Paul "to preach only Christ, and him crucified", hard as this may be.

As we do this, we face too the pain of what may seem to be the accusation of exclusivism; that we want others to be where we are, because we are glad to be there, and because we feel there is a uniqueness to what we have found there, or rather, to what God has revealed to us there. It may well be that our brother or sister of another faith is feeling the same thing at the same time, about their faith; we are so close, and yet so far, because we cannot be where he or she is. I am sure that is what our Muslim friends are often thinking. And yet, as John Taylor says: "To stop at disagreements is to lose faith in the Spirit's gift of communion and communication." And wherever we move on, he says, "it is the Lord's doing, and marvellous in our eyes".

Meeting in the Spirit

What we have experienced has been an "encounter in the Spirit". Let us conclude with an attempt to explain what this means.

I recall a small text that was given to me at the time of my ordination, from the book of Zechariah (4:10): "For who hath despised the day of small things?" Understanding this is crucial to the Christian life and to ministry. I did not know when I was given it how much it would be applicable for me to the area of interfaith encounter. Here we can begin with the people God offers, and in the way God offers. We do not need to feel tempted to wait for the "ideal". This may not be as we plan, as can be seen in the beginning of the story of our group, with that disastrous first meeting. We need not be concerned too with the number of people who come to our meetings. What is important is that they actually do meet in a real sense, small as their numbers may be. Often the sharpest moments of encounter are "when two or three are gathered together". This may be when nothing formal has been arranged at all. It is natural to look for "achievement", but it can prevent an open-endedness, to give freedom for the Spirit to act, and this requires time too, often years rather than months or weeks. Such can rarely happen on a one-off "dialogue meeting", which can be formally friendly and avoids the issues, or so confrontational that there is no actual meeting.

Nor need we seek out only the educated and those with official positions in another faith; our whole story reinforces this point. We also cannot expect to see all the results of these encounters. That applies to any area of Christian ministry, of course.

In a meeting of the kind I have described, very soon the partners catch something of the atmosphere. They are led to rethink some of the easy assumptions held about other faiths. Just as for the Christian it may be the first real meeting he or she has had with, say, an Asian of another faith, it may too be for the Muslim the first time to be with a believing and practising Christian who takes his or her faith seriously. Stereotypes are quickly broken down. About how we see other faiths: "Hindus do not take the material world seriously"; "Muslims are all fanatics"; "Muslim prayers are mechanical": and how they see us: "Christians are all permissive and immoral"; etc., etc.

The most important result of a meeting may not be what happens when we are together, but the ripple effect, as we go our separate ways, and witness to our own communities of our experience together. We witness then that Muslims or Christians are not all like this or that. This may affect attitudes to social issues too. I remember a student who said that one of the results of her meeting with those of other faiths and cultures was that she would never again allow racist remarks to go unchallenged as she tended to in the past.

Allowing the space for these unseen and usually unknown effects is allowing space for the Holy Spirit to blow where the Spirit wills.

Finally, and perhaps most crucial of all, we are confronted with our understanding of the Holy Spirit. Is it large enough to embrace all that we experience? Do we feel that what we are engaging in is the Spirit's work, and that the Spirit is the unseen third party in every such encounter, as John Taylor wrote in *The Go-between God*? These are, in other words, encounters in the Spirit. We, as Christians, do not own the Spirit. The Spirit is the enabler of all that is happening between us — leading us into all truth, breaking down the barriers between us, creating out of a dialogue between two parties a common search together for the truth that sets us free.

An appropriate way to conclude these reflections may be to meditate on some words from a hymn by Frederick Faber:

> There's a wideness in God's mercy
> Like the wideness of the sea;
> There's a kindness in his justice
> Which is more than liberty.

> For the love of God is broader
> Than the measures of man's mind;
> And the heart of the Eternal
> Is most wonderfully kind.

> But we make his love too narrow
> By false limits of our own;
> And we magnify his strictness
> With a zeal he will not own.

86

NOTES

London, Epworth Press, 1986, p.131.

Rome, 1969, p.157; quoted in *Can We Pray Together?*, an important booklet published by the British Council of Churches, 1983, p.20.

London, BCC, 1987.

London, SCM Press, 1981.

Voices of Varanasi, London, CMS, 1979, p.12.

Towards a New Relationship, *op. cit*, p.146.

Edited by George Appleton, Oxford, Oxford University Press, 1985.

By M. Hollings and E. Gullick, Great Wakering, Essex, Mayhew & Acrimmon, 1971.

Muslim Devotions, London, SPCK, 1961.

Towards a New Relationship, *op. cit.*, p.143.

See, for example, Alan Race, *Christians and Religious Pluralism*, London, SCM, 1983; Paul Knitter, *No Other Name?*, London, SCM, 1985; and *Towards a Theology for Inter-faith Dialogue*, CIO, 1984.

The Go-Between God, London, SCM, p.191.

Given at a conference at Tambaram, South India, and published in *International Review of Mission*, July 1988, pp.332-346.

Written in the preface to *Sandals to the Mosque*, Kenneth Cragg, London, SCM Press, 1959, p.9.

Op. cit., p.196.

Afterword:
Unexpected Encounters

The Satanic Verses

One of the fruits of what has been recorded earlier has been sustained friendship through recent strains. *The Satanic Verses* issue was about the book itself, but about much more than that. Since Salmaan Rushdie is both a born Muslim and a British citizen, it raised deep questions in Britain. Can the ruler of a foreign state, Ayatollah Khomeini, sentence to death a British citizen? Freedom to write within the law is a fundamental human right in Britain. But what are the rights of a minority Muslim community? And where is its voice?

In the background, much racism was unleashed. It became acceptable for educated white people to talk about Muslims in ways which, if they were about Pakistanis, would be against the Race Relations Act. The other way round, those who had chosen to live in British society, with all its comparative freedoms and opportunities, easily stereotyped it as a place of complete decadence and libertarianism, opening themselves to the obvious rejoinder, if you don't like it here, then go to one of your Muslim countries. The need for patient interpretation was never greater. And both Muslims and Christians involved in our meeting found themselves in this position.

One or two examples. Qazi read the whole of *The Satanic Verses*, with great personal pain, and listed the offending passages, to enable Christians to understand. He wrote a long and carefully phrased letter to the Ayatollah, explaining the situation in Britain. He mentioned that every country has its own rule of law, based on written or unwritten constitutions. The *fatwa*, based on Islamic laws and traditions, is irrevocable in an Islamic state. But it is advisable to respect the laws of other countries too. It would be appropriate to open doors to negotiations to re-establish good relations, based on Islamic teachings of goodwill and love. We learn from the Qur'an that every soul shall have a taste of death (3.185). Nor can a soul die except by Allah's Leave, the term being fixed as by writing (3.145). At the time this was a remarkable, conciliatory letter.

We were invited together to a meeting in the south of England, where the reading of our book had led to a wish to launch a Muslim-Christian dialogue group. The catalyst was the Salmaan Rushdie affair. The member of parliament was present and spoke of how he must represent all his constituents, of whatever faith. One problem throughout this period has been the fact that there is no Muslim amongst over 600 members of parliament. A Muslim spoke of how *Encounter in the Spirit* had impressed him because of the mutual sharing of pains. And sharing of pain and misunderstanding about *The Satanic Verses* was the centre of the meeting. Qazi advised: "Show them that you love them, they cannot then help but love you." The meeting was held in a church hall, proceeded to the local mosque, and ended with eating together in a Muslim home.

Less harmonious was an occasion when I was invited, through Muslim friends, to speak on *The Satanic Verses* as a Christian minister, at a meeting attended by almost a hundred Imams and leading Muslims. There was already much disunity and bad temper, and a feeling of powerlessness, expressed in earlier speeches. What was I to say? I prayed for the right words, thinking of the Holy Spirit's special gift in such situations! I expressed my great respect for Islam, and an understanding of how Muslims were feeling in the situation. I then made clear what I felt about a death threat from outside this country. I found half of the audience beginning to shout at me; but then as I grew alarmed, the other half began to shout at this half, for shouting at me! I went on to explain how I understood Islam asserted that Allah was the merciful one; and that my own understanding of God's nature was rooted in how Jesus showed that forgiveness lies at the heart of God. After some minutes I thankfully went back to my seat, and more and more divided speeches went on. Those sitting next to me thanked me for my understanding contribution. Their community was helpless, the British government was not going to give in, and the mood was one of general frustration.

In spite of such a distressing experience, maybe there were also some good things to come out of this whole affair. Muslims learnt much about standing up for themselves. And it was often church leaders, such as, for example, the Bishop of Bradford, who were found speaking alongside them, and saying they had a right to be heard. The affair showed how religion and culture are inextricably mixed within a faith such as Islam, and we cannot just neatly privatize religion, as many Western Christians tend to do. And the assertion of freedom of expression is important, but is not necessarily of ultimate value, as we often affirm. It is, in any case, limited in various ways already, by laws of libel, and slander, and pornography, and race relations. As I write, some previously long-banned films are being shown on television. And Muslims have had to think through carefully what it means to live as a minority, and to respect the law as a minority, and this is a long process for them. So much of their thinking applies to where Islam and the state are one. If this affair helped to begin these sorts of thinking from both sides, then perhaps it may not have the disastrous effect on Muslim-Christian relations that it looked at one time it might.

The Gulf war

One positive by-product of this tragedy has been increasing local attempts by Muslims and Christians to get together. In Birmingham there was a joint statement from a Muslim Liaison Committee and the presidents of the Birmingham Council of Christian Churches. This expressed awareness of growing racism and the incidents of verbal and physical abuse against Muslims in Birmingham and elsewhere, which raised "the spectre of a reopened chasm across the Mediterranean between the Muslim world and Christendom... It is clear that this is not a war between Muslims and Christians, but in the Middle East people are remembering the Crusades, and in Europe people are remembering the move of Islam into formerly Christian lands... The longer this war lasts, the greater is the danger of us being sucked into the prison of these medieval stereotypes. As Christians and Muslims, we must continue to insist that we are all God's creatures; we must continue to resist the temptation to label the other as the enemy."

I was interviewed by the BBC at the time, and asked to comment on a quotation in a quality newspaper that the largest forces of Christendom were ranged against the largest forces of Islam since the crusades. A somewhat simplistic view, with only Saudis, Egyptians and Syrians with the "alliance", and the Iraqi foreign minister and several hundred thousand Iraqis being Christians.

In this situation, to pray publicly together seemed the appropriate action. This was not to do nothing, but to do something of deep significance. We had a joint vigil on 14 January 1991, just before the UN deadline ran out. It ended at midnight, after three hours of prayer. It made linkages as we prayed for forgiveness for the past, and looked at the whole of the Middle East, including Palestine and Lebanon as well as the Gulf. Muslim friends spoke, and recited the Qur'an, and prayed for peace. It was striking particularly for the many Christians who had not experienced such Muslim prayer before. They were converted from "stereotypes", and that can only be a gain as we look ahead to what has to be done in Muslim-Christian relations in the future.

I describe one more meeting. This was in a community centre and involved Zaheer. His sensitivity had already come over to an international group of friends with me — from Africa, Scandinavia and Britain. In answer to a question about the meaning of a minaret, he had said it was to show the oneness of God — he is not two or four or five, but one! He smiled at me, with a twinkle in his eye, taking special care not to insult our seeing God as Three as well as One!

We then had a long discussion on the Gulf war and its aftermath. There was real listening. It was Zaheer who said that future peace would depend on all true Muslims, Christians and Jews — and he is always inclusive here — standing together, with the resources of their traditions. They should be people of faith first, and politicians second. At the end he asked me to pray. I felt ashamed that I did not mention Jesus at all in my prayer, when he came to pray, and used his name, along with Muhammad and Moses. Peace was upon all of them. An example of real sensitivity! The content of his prayer moved me, and indeed all of us. Recognizing the presence of Africans, he prayed for those starving and being forgotten in that continent, again something I had not thought of. Turning to the Middle East, he prayed for all, Muslims, Christians and Jews, "that those who have suffered so much and died so terribly, Jews, Christians and Muslims, in Palestine, Lebanon, Kuwait and Iraq, may now be enjoying a better life with God himself". As Christians we could not but be struck by the assurance of hope.

I had been horrified by two pictures in a Sunday newspaper, of two Iraqis. One had been incinerated in his tank, a result of allied bombing. We were praying in hope for him, and his hope is only beyond this life, as also for so many Kurds killed mercilessly by fellow Muslims in the weeks that followed. The other photo was of an Iraqi soldier with a haunted and desperate look, holding up his hands, begging to be captured. Our joint prayer must be that he and his family may be able to enjoy a better life on this earth, and not only in eternity.

I hope that the re-issue of this book may encourage Christians and Muslims, wherever they are, to work with each other and not against each other, and indeed with people of all faiths and none, to realize that better life, particularly for the poor amongst them, who are the special concern of the scriptures of both faiths, and of the teaching of both Jesus and Muhammad.

Easter 1991   ANDREW WINGATE